Council Over Pope?

Council Over Pope?

Towards a Provisional Ecclesiology

Francis Oakley

Herder and Herder

1969
HERDER AND HERDER NEW YORK
232 Madison Avenue, New York, N.Y. 10016

Library of Congress Catalog Card Number: 73–80871

Contents

TO
CLAIRE-ANN

Preface

This book was conceived and mapped out in its main outlines long before several recent papal actions underlined the importance of the complex issues with which it seeks to grapple. The first chapter was completed by the time Pope Paul issued his "new Credo". The bulk of the book was written before the appearance of the encyclical *Humanae vitae* and its transformation of the problem of papal authority from a dark cloud on the horizon of ecumenism to a question of conscience for vast numbers of Catholics and a matter of immediate concern to those economists and politicians whose task it is to juggle with the bleak equations of rising populations and deepening poverty in the developing countries.

Perhaps the best way to convey some sense of the general thrust of the book is to say that it represents an historian's attempt to open up a middle way between the paths chosen by Charles Davis and Gregory Baum respectively—the one clearcut and admirably firm, but open, some would say, to the charge of excessive literalism; the other somewhat fuzzy and overgrown and marred, so Davis would have us believe, by a loyalist's proclivity for institutional wishful thinking. Doubtless there will be some, perhaps many, to whom any such attempt is likely to appear as an absurdity, an exercise in futility, by its very nature doomed to failure. Nor can I myself pretend to be sanguine about the particular prospects awaiting my own attempt. But neither do I find it possible to relinquish the conviction that the current direction of papal policy—with all the misery it is likely to entail for the poor, the scrupulous, the simple, the uninformed, the victims of governmental inertia in developing countries burdened with a Cath-

9

olic establishment, and so on—has rendered it doubly imperative that such an attempt indeed be made, whatever the theological obstacles it must surmount and whatever the psychological barriers it will undoubtedly encounter.

The book, then, is something more than an historical study. But the case it makes pivots upon an historical argument, and it is an extended piece of historical analysis that constitutes its first part. I emphasize this fact without apology, not unaware, moreover, that a sensitivity to the historical dimension of reality has rarely been a distinguishing feature of Catholic ecclesiological thinking. Even in the recent past few Catholic institutions of higher education have been willing to give to the study of Church history the type of honor and precedence accorded so readily and with such tiresome insistence to scholastic philosophy and theology. As a result, it remains paradoxical but true to say that in a century during which a conviction of his own essential historicity has sunk deep into the consciousness of man, the patterns of thought characteristic of an extraordinary number of our Catholic theologians have remained persistently, adamantly, even aggressively a-historical. For this insensitivity to the historical, however, and for the concomitant willingness to take refuge on critical points in a tendentious manipulation of historical data, a heavy price has been and is still being paid. And that price, I fear, is a major factor in the grave crisis of authority which racks the Catholic world today.

I wish to acknowledge my indebtedness to the President and Trustees of Williams College for a grant from the Class of 1900 Fund towards the cost of preparing the manuscript for the press, to Mrs. Nancy MacFadyen of the Williams College Library for the efficiency, promptness and good humor with which invariably she handled my repeated demands on the Interlibrary Loan Service, to my friend Martin Griffin, of the Yale History Department, for his numerous and characteristic kindnesses to me, and to my

10

wife and children for their willingness to endure, over the long and beckoning summer months, the dawn to dusk preoccupation of an unseasonably abstracted husband and father.

F.O.

Williamstown, Massachusetts
January, 1969

The Matter of Relevance

(a) Situational

By the time I sat down to write these words [1] it had become evident, if not indeed to all Catholics, at least to those anxious to discern the direction of the current that was sweeping them away from ancient ecclesial moorings, that the benign stream of reform liberated by the efforts of the late Pope John XXIII had deepened, suddenly (it seemed) and disconcertingly, into a torrent of revolutionary dimensions. There could be no mistaking this fact—least of all by anyone who had made the effort to mark the drift of public opinion in the Church or who had struggled to keep his footing amid the surge of theological speculation flooding from the presses of "religious" and "secular" publishers alike and despite the disconcerting undertow of papal and episcopal alarm that accompanied it. The Church was sliding into revolutionary turmoil, the days of the liberal reformers seemed numbered, and maneuver though they might in the hope of precipitating a premature Thermidor, conservatives—and along with them the rest of us—seemed destined first to undergo the therapeutic rigors of a Jacobin phase.

And yet, as I write these words, I am sensible of the fact that to vast numbers of my fellow Catholics, should they read this book, they would savor only of fantasy. I can well understand why this should be so. In many regions in the United States—as in many parts of the world—local ecclesiastical life presents to the casual

1. June 24, 1968, a week before Pope Paul issued his "new Credo".

observer an astonishingly placid surface.[2] In these areas, if ecclesiastical feathers may often have been ruffled while the Second Vatican Council was still in session, the apocalyptic winds of change seem, since then, to have dwindled to the gentlest of institutional breezes. In such areas the traditional patterns of thought and the old and familiar ways of doing things have shown a remarkable resiliency. Liturgical renewal has been reduced to a dismal business of rubrical manipulation, ecumenism has been domesticated successfully within the mannerist niceties of chancery propriety, the priesthood of all believers has fallen a silent victim on the high road back to clericalist normalcy, and the new dignity of the laity has been successfully defused by making it a matter for abstract homiletic exhortation—transformed thereby into something understandably remote from anything recognizable by the average layman as pertaining to the truly real world outside.

In such areas, again, one can almost sense the relief with which attention has been returned, once more, to matters of endearingly pre-Conciliar vintage: the management of parish finances ("prudence"), the proliferation of church-buildings ("generosity"), the evasion of social issues ("religion"), the worship of the institution ("loyalty"), the preaching of a sturdy Semi-Pelagianism ("othodoxy"), the collection of sacramental statistics ("spiritual stock-taking"), the socialization of children into antique ecclesial norms ("religious education"), and ("lay apostolate") the promotion of religious societies—so many of them emasculated parochial bodies that are little more than bureaucratic fictions, paper dragons, phantom battalions filed periodically on the appropriate form in the cabinets of diocesan chanceries, cheek by jowl, no doubt, with those other shadowy organizations whose ghostly activities long have haunted the purlieus of the Catholic episcopal imagination. In such areas, moreover, stimulated perhaps by the unwelcome degree of press-attention accorded in recent years to things ecclesiastical, little

2. New England is certainly one of these regions.

effort is spared in trying to represent the Church, once more, as a coherent, smooth-running—even monolithic—organization, one that pivots at Rome on a well-oiled central administrative apparatus responsive immediately to the most delicate of papal nudges at the controls; depicting it, in other words, very much as what its enemies once condemned, its sympathizers once deplored, and its apologists once sought to excuse. The best of Blanshard, as it were, and *paleo*-Blanshard at that!

Even in such areas, however, closer observation will reveal a few straws in the wind. Attendance at Sunday Mass may not have declined but the practice of regular confession apparently has. So, too, attendance at once popular extra-liturgical devotions. So, too, for good or ill, the amount of attention paid to clerical attempts at moral guidance. On the birth control issue, Pope Paul could declare in 1966 that "the magisterium is not in doubt," but many lay people obviously were, and the public silence of most of the parochial clergy witnessed to their own profound unease on the matter. Even if *Humanae vitae* succeeds in settling that unease (and it is hard to believe that it will), it seems unlikely to determine the attitudes of the bulk of those lay people whom it most directly affects. Abject obedience to clerical prescriptions— at least in what are regarded as purely "religious" issues—if still very evident among the older people, is clearly on its way out. The "priest-worship" of the past is losing its devotees, the vestal virgin seems doomed to go the way of the sacred prostitute, and the periodic announcement in the popular press of yet another priest-nun wedding tends now to evoke among lay people human sympathy rather than instinctive revulsion, a certain wry humor rather than a sense of outrage.

Hostility in the face of change, uneasiness, insecurity, foot-dragging—all of these undoubtedly persist, but even a scrutiny of the local scene gives one reason to believe that behind the inarticulacy and conservatism characteristic of so much of lay Catholic life, a residual conscience has been stirred. A mood is being shaped, it would seem, that will lead many in the long run to

15

abandon the security of heteronomy and the inanities of the old ethic of obedience, in order to risk the perils of autonomy and the agonies of personal moral decision.[3] And once one turns from the strongholds of apathy and bastions of conservatism on the local scene to the situation in the Church at large, it becomes clear that what in one context may savor somewhat of fantasy, in another presents itself with all the force of sober reality. Let it be admitted, then, that the Church is caught up in a revolution, a revolution affecting every aspect of its life but focusing in particular upon three fundamental issues: the practical range and theoretical implications of institutional reform, ecclesiastical authority and the meaning of Church unity, the nature of the Christian faith.

These questions are intimately related one to another and it would, of course, be improper to suggest that the fathers of the Second Vatican Council were concerned exclusively with the first. But if their subsequent behavior is any adequate guide to their thinking, it seems clear that many of the bishops, despite the efforts of their *periti* (or perhaps *because* of them),[4] viewed the conciliar decrees for which they voted from the standpoint of a persistent externality.[5] It also seems fair to say that the subsequent and widespread demand for reform of the Church "in head and members" has outpaced both in its urgency and in its dimensions anything envisaged by many of those "liberal" bishops who assented so blithely in conciliar decrees the radical potentialities of which they seem often to have missed. And as the gulf widens between the soaring Utopian visions of radical and wide-ranging reform and the piecemeal institutional tinkering that seems to mark the limit of what, under present conditions, it is realistic to hope for, there is developing a growing unease about the very

3. Because it focusses so directly on a "gut issue" affecting so many people and because it has received so much publicity, Pope Paul's encyclical on family limitation will undoubtedly serve to accelerate this process.

4. Cf. the remarks of Charles Davis, *A Question of Conscience* (London and New York, 1967), pp. 127-128.

5. As his "Credo" of June 30, 1968, makes amply clear, the same is true of Pope Paul who approved those decrees.

possibility of institutional reform, an unease deepening in some circles into a more fundamental disenchantment with the very church-institution itself—a shift, as it were, from the accommodating categories of gradualism to the bleak perspectives of abolitionism.

For some people this situation may well lead, as it did most notably in the case of Charles Davis, to a clean break with the Church, to an open rejection of its claims, to a concomitant disclaimer of membership in it. But, as Davis himself notes, one has to accord a certain importance to visible ecclesiastical structures in order to find it necessary to reject them. "It was because I was a moderate rather than a radical theologian that I was led to break with the Church."[6] As a radical, presumably, without formal repudiation of his confessional allegiance he would have been able to work out his destiny in the context of the "free church" or "underground church" movement, a spontaneous movement which, rejecting the very idea of the Church as an "identifiable sacred organism", cuts across traditional denominational boundaries and embarks in independence of all institutional structures upon "the quest for the authentic Christian community".[7]

The understanding of the Church reflected in this movement goes a long way, in its extreme form, towards dissolving "any need for the sort of church idea which would interpret itself as something more or something else than the life of man in the world".[8] And even in its less extreme versions it has certainly called into question the predominantly institutional or organizational conception of Church unity so characteristic of Catholic thinking in the past. I know of no statistics indicating the extent of Catholic involvement in this "free church" movement. If its geographical spread is impressive, its numerical strength almost certainly is not. But it is noteworthy that its ranks should include

6. *A Question of Conscience*, p. 168.
7. Rosemary Ruether, "Schism of Consciousness," *Commonweal*, May 31, 1968, 328-329.
8. *Ibid.*, 330.

17

some of the most committed and theologically gifted Catholics of our era.

Because of this, there is a certain legitimacy in the recent observation that "the schism many have feared within Catholicism already exists" even if "it is less visible and more subtle than may have been expected. The ancient outward forms persist, but there is a great divergence among those perceiving them." [9] That divergence reflects the existence "within" the Church of truly radical disagreement concerning the very nature and import of the Christian faith. In this connection, Rosemary Ruether has asserted that "never in the history of Christianity has there existed, within the formal boundaries of a single ecclesiastical institution, poles of interpretation which share so little of what is termed 'a common faith' ".[10]

If her exaggeration is real, it is nonetheless pardonable. The ecclesiastical hierarchy may wish to decree otherwise, but a reasonably empirical appraisal of the post-conciliar Church reveals it to be a church disrupted by its own attempts at reform, a church divided in its own attempts at self-understanding, a church uncertain of the meaning, the status and the consequences of its own faith. Indeed, it is the very wish of the hierarchy to decree otherwise, to legislate a solution, to act as a collective Canute ordering the tides to turn back, that threatens increasingly to precipitate a dramatic showdown.[11]

For if it is true that for all Christians "the problem of God is more important than the problem of the Church" it is also true that for most Catholics "the latter often stands in the way of the former".[12] And the problem of the Church today is, in its most

9. Mary Daly, "Dispensing with Trivia," *Commonweal*, May 31, 1968, 325.

10. *Ibid.*, 327.

11. Cf. Davis's remark: "My relation with authority did contribute much to my leaving the Church. Neither the Holy See nor the bishops directly blocked my activities, but they helped considerably in destroying my faith. What they helped to destroy for me was the credibility of the Church." *A Question of Conscience*, p. 46.

12. Hans Küng, *The Church*, trans. Ray and Rosaleen Ockenden (London and New York, 1968), p. xiii.

obviously practical dimensions, the problem of the locus and nature of ecclesiastical authority. At the very heart of the crisis with which individual Catholics will increasingly have to grapple stand the traditional jurisdictional pretensions and magisterial claims of the clerical hierarchy. And again, in practical terms, despite the gargantuan labors of Vatican II, despite the subsequent papal attempts at curial reform, despite the insistent, omnipresent and (alas!) empty rhetoric of collegiality—despite all of these and more—to say this is still to an astonishing degree to say that at the heart of the crisis confronting the Church today stands the papal primacy as officially conceived and currently exercised. It has long been recognized, of course, and admitted by Pope Paul himself, that the Roman primacy stands out as perhaps the greatest obstacle in the way of reuniting the separated Christian churches.[13] But it is only in the last two or three years that it has become at all common for troubled Catholics themselves to admit that it is the traditional conception and current exercise of that primacy which, more than any other *single* factor, is serving for them to erode the credibility of the Catholic church itself.[14]

(b) Personal

The Church at large, then, is plunging into revolutionary turmoil, it is torn progressively by an updated variety of schism, it is undergoing increasingly an acute crisis of faith. This being so, it seems reasonable to predict that the situation will make more

13. As if to emphasize this point, Pope Paul issued his "new Credo" at the very moment when a Catholic delegation was on its way to enter into discussions with the general assembly of the World Council of Churches at Uppsala.

14. Because of John Cogley's distinguished career in Catholic journalism, his reaction to *Humanae vitae* is a particularly striking illustration of this point. Admitting that "the Pope's encyclical, for me at least, opened a Pandora's box", he decided to discontinue the syndicated column of his which had been appearing in about thirty diocesan newspapers. "Cogley's Last Column," *The National Catholic Reporter*, August 28, 1968, 8.

and more harsh demands upon all of us—shaking former loyalties, threatening old friendships, dimming familiar memories. Confronted personally with the urgencies of this state of affairs, individual Catholics will struggle to find their own footing in accordance with their own temperaments and their individual psychological, moral and intellectual resources. As an historian, it is understandable that I, myself, should turn for enlightenment to a renewed scrutiny of Church history. But that I should turn in particular to the history of the *medieval* Church is certainly less fashionable and perhaps less readily comprehensible. At a moment when the turn from the closed worlds of the Mannings and MacIntyres to the infinite universes of the Rahners and Ruethers is reaching a point of truly Copernican decision, the medieval experience, once so stiflingly eulogized in Catholic circles, is no longer exactly at a premium. And, after the confusions and disappointments consequent upon the recent conciliar and synodal experiences, it may seem even more peculiar that I should turn, in particular, to the history of the medieval general councils.

Certainly those whose anti-institutionalism is such that they see no need "for the sort of church idea which would interpret itself as something more or something else than the life of man in the world" or who would "dissolve the institutional reference of the word 'church'" [15] will, no doubt, find my particular concerns, if not incomprehensible, at least redundant. But, then, I, myself, find it impossible to share their own indifference to institutions and to organizational structures. Like very many others, I would want to accord considerably greater importance to the church-institution than Rosemary Ruether, for example, seems willing to grant. And not only for negative reasons—though these themselves are very persuasive. "The stuff out of which society and all its formations are made is human meaning externalized in human activity." [16] It is institutions, after all, which

15. Rosemary Ruether, "Schism of Consciousness," 329-330.
16. Peter Berger, *The Sacred Canopy: Elements of a Sociological Theory of Religion* (New York, 1967), p. 8.

embody and convey meanings across the hostility of time. Without the persistence of the church-institution and the meanings (and counter-meanings) it has succeeded in conveying, the type of spiritual SDS movement envisaged by some of the apologists of the underground church would be inconceivable.[17] There is a sense in which the existence of this movement—like that of its secular counterpart—is parasitic. Its very identity is defined, and to a remarkable degree, in contradistinction to the institutional Church.[18] It *needs* the institution. Just as the institution, in turn, needs it. For if the free or underground church movement is to make a real contribution to the common well-being of *all* it will surely do so only in continuing tension and dialectic with a surviving institutional Church. In this respect one would do well to recall Martin Marty's comment that there would be something wrong with the concern for the common well-being shown by those whom he calls "the ethicalists" if it were extended only to the "poor outsider" and excluded compassion for one's own "slow-moving, fellow believer".[19]

If one has arrived at the conclusion that the Catholic church in its traditional form and in its present functioning has come to constitute "a serious obstacle to the development of Christian faith and mission"[20] (and many Catholics, however reluctantly, have done so), then radical change in the institution should

17. SDS: Students for a Democratic Society. I do not think the analogy is an unfair one. Ruether herself claims that "the Freedom Movement has become the paradigm for ecclesiology in the American theology of our times", *The Church Against Itself* (London and New York, 1968), p. 206; cf. her comparison of the free church with "other movements, such as the 'free press' and the 'free university' which are similarly moving outside present power structures to find more authentic ways of doing things", "Schism of Consciousness," 329-330.

18. Thus its designation as a "free church" or "underground church" movement.

19. *National Catholic Reporter,* June 26, 1968, 8; he has returned to this theme in a more recent article: "A Warning to Catholic Extremists," *America,* August 31, 1968, 124.

20. Davis, *A Question of Conscience,* p. 170; cf. George J. Hafner, "A New Style of Christianity," *Commonweal,* May 31, 1968, 333: "I have come to believe that the principal obstacle to Christianity in the world today is the Christian Church."

21

surely remain an urgent priority. This change, it is true, would involve for some an outright rejection of the absolutist claims traditional to the clerical hierarchy and a firm insistence on the secondary nature of all formally commissioned ecclesiastical authority, on the provisional nature of all church structures, on the relative nature of all dogmatic formulations. But even if it did, those who feel this way should perceive that, given the degree of "spiritual mutilation" attendant upon so much Catholic indoctrination,[21] it is only with the help of the church institution, paradoxically enough, that many devoted Catholics will be able to bring themselves to accept that rejection. It is the institution, and the institution alone, that can demythologize itself. It is the institution, and the institution alone, that can place itself fully under the judgment of the Gospel and free its members from the oppressive weight of its former dominion.

In the great crisis that confronts us, institutional change, then, cannot simply be dismissed as mere "internal housekeeping". It remains an urgent imperative. And the exigencies of this change raise practical and theoretical problems of the greatest complexity and of the utmost sensitivity. This being so, it is my belief—and the belief that undergirds this book—that in our time of troubles the history of the later-medieval church has something of importance to say to us; that the scandal and schism engendered by its decadence and the great conciliar effort mounted to overcome that schism have an immediate relevance to the crisis that has overtaken the Church today in what was expected, ironically enough, to have been its moment of renewed glory.[22]

21. For some cogent remarks on this point, see Daly, "Dispensing with Trivia," 323-324.

22. This expectation was not, of course, shared by conservatives. As Davis, Berger and others have pointed out, the conservative appraisal of the radical implications of *aggiornamento* seems to have been well founded, *A Question of Conscience,* p. 29; *The Sacred Canopy,* p. 169.

(c) Historical

When Pope John XXIII, in 1959, first announced to a small assembly of close associates his intention of summoning a general council his request for advice was met, to his surprise, with silence. He, himself, was later to call it "a devout and impressive silence", but if the subsequent behavior of the clerics who staff the Congregations of the Roman *curia* can be taken as a guide, it seems instead to have been the silence of incredulity.[23]

There were good reasons for this incredulity. General councils had always been exceptional occurrences in the life of the Church. It had become customary at Rome to recognize only twenty of the great synods that had assembled over the course of history as having been in trust general or ecumenical councils of the universal Church. In over nineteen hundred years these twenty councils had been in actual session for a meagre total of little more than thirty years. Moreover, if the definition by the First Vatican Council of the papal primacy in jurisdiction and infallibility in teaching had not itself been enough to make the extraordinary and cumbersome conciliar mechanism a redundancy, then surely the recovery of papal prestige in the last hundred years and the marked acceleration in the pace of administrative centralization that accompanied it had succeeded in doing so.[24]

The initial reaction of the Roman *curia* to the unexpected reactivation of what most of its members seem to have taken to be an ecclesiological museum piece was, then, one of incredulity deepening swiftly into consternation. But on this, as on so many other matters, curialist sentiment was not matched by sentiment in the Church at large. When the Pope's intentions were made

23. See Xavier Rynne, *Letters from Vatican City* (New York, 1963), pp. 1 ff.
24. Rynne, *Letters,* pp. 25 ff., 48 ff.

23

known and his determination became clear, the general response, if somewhat puzzled, was unquestionably favorable. This response, in turn, spawned something of a renaissance of interest in conciliar history. Given the pre-eminence of the papacy in the modern Church, that interest understandably enough focussed less on the great ecumenical councils of Christian antiquity, in which the Roman pontiffs had not played a predominant role, than on Trent and Vatican I, the two modern assemblies in which they had and which might, therefore, be expected to serve as models for the projected council. And interest focussed least of all on the three councils of the later Middle Ages—Pisa (1409), Constance (1414–18) and Basel (1431–49)—for these had clearly to be regarded as extraordinary assemblies, the products of a period of crisis, their procedures and activities in no way normative for the subsequent life of the Church.[25]

This attitude is reflected in Hans Küng's *The Council, Reform and Union*—perhaps the most widely read of all the programmatic reformist works to have been written under the stimulus of Pope John's convocation of the new council.[26] It is reflected even more clearly in the three brief conciliar histories which appeared on the eve of that council and which enjoyed a wide circulation throughout the English-speaking world and beyond—those written by the distinguished Church historians, Jedin, Dvornik and Hughes.[27] As these historians themselves indicate, the trouble with those late-medieval councils was that, meeting at a time of grave crisis in the life of the Church and confronted by widespread ecclesiastical corruption, by schism and by the aftermath

25. Though Pope John XXIII's choice of name with its possible implication that the previous John XXIII had been merely an anti-pope had sponsored a brief flurry of interest in Pisa and Constance. See K. A. Fink, "Zur Beurteilung des Grossen Abendländischen Schismas," *Zeitschrift für Kirchengeschichte*, LXXIII (1962), 336-338.

26. The book scarcely mentions Constance at all.

27. Hubert Jedin, *Ecumenical Councils of the Catholic Church*, trans. Ernest Graf (London and New York, 1960); Francis Dvornik, *The Ecumenical Councils* (New York, 1961); Philip Hughes, *The Church in Crisis: A History of the General Councils 325–1870* (New York, 1961).

of schism, they tried "to introduce radical changes into the constitution of the Church" (Dvornik, p. 78). Their mistake was that of having made "questionable concessions to Conciliar theory" (Jedin, p. 125), a theory which asserted that the pope was not an absolute monarch but in some sense a constitutional ruler, that he possessed a merely ministerial authority delegated to him for the good of the Church, that the final jurisdictional power in the Church lay, therefore, not with the pope but with the whole body of the faithful or with their representatives gathered together in a general council.[28] Endorsement of that theory by the fathers of Constance in the famous decree *Haec sancta* (1415) had made possible, it is true, the elimination of the rival claimants to the papacy and the termination of a scandalous schism which had endured for almost fifty years and resisted all previous attempts to end it. But in the view of these modern historians (and in this they are representative of standard modern Catholic thinking), concessions to the Conciliar theory have still to be regarded as questionable, because that theory was a "dangerous and erroneous doctrine" (Dvornik, p. 79), one which threatened "the rightful position" of the papacy (*ibid.*, p. 74) and which could never "fit into the hierarchical structure of the Church" (Jedin, p. 176). Thus, although Hughes is willing to call Constance "one of the great turning points of the history of the Church" (even if it did many "things impossible to harmonize with the tradition"—pp. 172–3), he accords it no more space in his book than he gives to the Fifth Lateran Council (1512–17)—an abortive assembly, the ecumenicity of which was questioned at Trent and which managed under papal domination to sidestep the most pressing problems of the day.

Of course, in a sense this is understandable enough. After three quasi-revolutionary councils functioning under what Dvornik called "the shadow of Conciliar theory", the Lateran council

28. The theory was in fact a good deal more complex than this simplified description might suggest. See below, ch. 2, pp. 61 ff.

marked a return to something approaching the pattern set by the great papal councils of the twelfth and thirteenth centuries—a return, that is, to a state of affairs approximating more closely to the modern Roman Catholic vision of what constitutes ecclesiological normalcy. The vogue of Conciliar theory among the fathers of Constance may have made possible the restoration of unity to the Church, but if Constance succeeded in ending the schism, it failed to achieve its related goal of reform in head and members, and, certainly, despite the assembly of subsequent councils at Siena and Basel, it sponsored no constitutional revolution in the Church. At Basel, moreover, the excesses of the radical Conciliarist majority led finally to the disaffection of some of its own most eminent supporters, to the triumph of Pope Eugenius IV and of the papalist party, and to the subsequent decline in the fortunes of Conciliar theory. If that theory managed to survive the Fifth Lateran Council and the Council of Trent (and it did so most notably in France where it lay at the heart of *theological* Gallicanism), it survived only as an ecclesiological tradition that came increasingly to be branded as heterodox. The sympathy shown towards it in the eighteenth century by the Febronians in Germany and the Josephines in Austria [29] did little to restore its fortunes in the market place of orthodoxy, and its endorsement by Old Catholic theologians in the late-nineteenth century did even less.[30] In any case, Vatican I's definitions of papal primacy and papal infallibility seemed to leave Catholic historians little choice but to treat the Conciliar movement as a revolutionary episode in the life of the Church, and Catholic theologians no alternative but to regard Conciliar theory as a dead issue, an ecclesiological fossil, something lodged deep in the lower carboniferous of the dogmatic geology.

29. See M. O'Callaghan, *New Catholic Encyclopedia*, V, s.v. "Febronianism," and F. Maass, *ibid.*, VII, s.v. "Josephinism."

30. See Pontien Polman, "Historical Background of Old Catholicism," *Concilium* (Glen Rock, New Jersey, 1965), VII, pp. 159-167.

In 1908, as a result, the editors of the *Catholic Encyclopedia* did not even deem it necessary to include in that work an article on Conciliarism. The subject was given some attention under the heading of "Gallicansim", but the author of that article did not hesitate to make the prevailing sentiment of his day abundantly clear. "Stricken to death, as a free opinion, by the Council of the Vatican", he said,

[theological] Gallicanism could survive only as a heresy; the Old Catholics have endeavoured to keep it alive under this form. Judged by the paucity of the adherents whom they have recruited—daily becoming fewer in Germany and Switzerland, it seems very evident that the historical evolution of these ideas has reached its completion.[31]

When one turns to the *New Catholic Encyclopedia,* published just last year, and to the article entitled "Conciliarism (Theology of)" one finds nothing to gainsay this judgment. The article in question was written at some point after the promulgation in November 1964 of *Lumen gentium,* Vatican II's *Dogmatic Constitution on the Church.* Its tone is not strident. Reference is made to *Lumen gentium.* We are urged not to regard the Conciliarists as "formal heretics" and to "remember that they did not have the same theological armory that exists today". Nevertheless, we are still told that these men *did* embrace "a doctrine alien to the Catholic faith", that Conciliarism is essentially "a false theory about the possessor of supreme authority in the Church", that "its fundamental error"—clearly expressed in the decree *Haec sancta*—"is that it attributes a supreme power of jurisdiction to a general assembly of bishops who are acting independently of the pope", for, the author insists, "there cannot be an ecumenical council [properly so called] without the active participation of

31. A Degart, in *The Catholic Encyclopedia,* VI, s.v. "Gallicanism," p. 355.

the pope, at least by way of approving the council's decisions." [32]

The attitude, then, has not changed. The point of view expressed in 1967, as in 1908, is Ultramontane. It is the point of view, some would argue, that the Council of Florence endorsed in 1439 and the Fifth Lateran Council in 1516.[33] It is the point of view that Dom Cuthbert Butler described as having triumphed at Vatican I and as having become, thereafter, synonymous with orthodoxy. It is a point of view, nevertheless, that one would not have expected to find reiterated in 1967 so forcefully and in such absolute terms. And for two reasons.

In the first place, because the scholarly labors of the last few decades, especially in the history of medieval canon law, have made it unambiguously clear that the Conciliar theory which dominated the great fifteenth-century councils was neither as recent in its origins nor as revolutionary in its claims, nor as rapid in its demise as it was formerly usual to assume. In the second place, because one of the most fascinating by-products of John XXIII's convocation of the Second Vatican Council was Paul de Vooght's direction of attention once more to the dogmatic status of the Conciliarist decree *Haec sancta,* the subsequent refurbishing in some theological circles of the Conciliarist image, and Hans Küng's blunt insistence in 1962 that the dogmatically binding character of that decree "is not to be evaded" by the Church today. These claims, predictably, have stirred considerable controversy. A few scholars have been inclined to endorse them. Others, however, have found it impossible to accept them *in toto* or have rejected them outright. Most have simply ignored them. But even if such claims had no impact at all on the Conciliar constitutions and decrees of Vatican II, the debate about

32. L. Örsy, *New Catholic Encyclopedia,* IV, s.v. "Conciliarism (Theology of)." It should be noted that in the accompanying article, "Conciliarism (History of)," Professor Brian Tierney of Cornell University, who has made a fundamental and distinguished contribution to our understanding of Conciliar theory, presents a much more subtly nuanced analysis.

33. But see below, ch. 3, p. 91.

them still continues and its outcome is uncertain. What is not uncertain, however, is the fact that at no time since the early sixteenth century has the Conciliar theory seemed as viable on ecclesiological option to Catholic theologians as it does today. In this respect the legacy of Constance has proved to be a much less negative and much more vital one than most of those writing on the eve of Vatican II seem even to have imagined.

And not only vital, but also relevant—relevant particularly to this post-conciliar period and to the deepening crisis of authority that has accompanied it. Unlike the conservative minority, the progressive leadership at Vatican II (and the majority which was willing to follow it) believed it possible to combine the traditional stress on the essentially unchanging nature of defined Catholic truth with a recognition of the fundamental historicity of man and with the flexibility and openness to change which conditions in the modern world had forced upon their attention as unquestionably necessary. They also believed it possible (and the point is not unrelated) to combine the modern view of papal authority, in its final Ultramontane plenitude, with the less juridical and more collegial emphasis to which modern biblical and patristic scholarship has pointed with increasing insistence.

Pope Paul's "new Credo" and his encyclical *Humanae vitae* stand only as the most dramatic of the events that are conspiring to prove them wrong. And as the post-conciliar Church slides into revolutionary turmoil, into widening schism and into a deepening crisis of faith, the barriers that hitherto have stood between us and a meaningful appreciation of the Conciliarist era (still very much unknown territory to most Catholics) have begun to crumble. Because of this, it is my belief that a strong case can now be made for liberating the Conciliarist ecclesiology from the doctrinal limbo to which Catholic theologians, until very recently, have unhesitatingly assigned it. Basic, however, to any attempt to assess the validity of the claims made by the "new Conciliarists", and prior to any of the dogmatic shortcuts so long

29

and so destructively fashionable, must necessarily be an historical analysis of the Conciliarist decrees, of the Conciliar theory which stood behind them, of the Conciliar movement in general, and of the events which ensured its rise to prominence and served to precipitate its subsequent decline. Part I of the book addresses itself, therefore, to this task. In Part II, the claims of the revisionists will be evaluated, an attempt will be made to assess the relevance of their claims to the problem of authority today, and some suggestions will be advanced concerning the possible consequences of those claims for the Church of tomorrow.

PART I

Historical

CHAPTER 1

The Great Schism and
the Conciliar Movement

(a) Historical Fundamentals

By an archaic insight since calcified into a pedagogic norm, it has become customary among historians to divide the history of the medieval Church at a particular moment of great drama, and not uncommon for them to endow the period preceding that moment with the qualities of zeal, vigor and hope, while burdening the period following upon it with the attributes of weariness, decadence and despair. This approach has a good deal to recommend it. The moment in question—the "outrage of Anagni" in September 1303—was a moment not only of drama but also of great irony. It witnessed the abject humiliation of a pope at the hands of mercenaries in French pay and under French leadership, and not of any pope but of the great Pope Boniface VIII himself. And less than a year previously he had issued the famous bull *Unam sanctam* reiterating in uncompromising terms of unprecedented clarity the claim that the temporal authority should be subjected to the spiritual.[1] Clearly a great turning point in the history of the medieval papacy.

The aftermath of Anagni was the transfer of the papacy from Rome to Avignon on the borders of the French kingdom. And the residence at Avignon, regarded by many at the time and since

---

1. Brian Tierney, *The Crisis of Church and State: 1050–1300* (Englewood Cliffs, New Jersey, 1964), pp. 188-191, reprints a translation of *Unam Sanctam* and of an eyewitness account of the "outrage".

as an appalling scandal, was compared by the disaffected rigorist wing of the Franciscans, the Fraticelli, with the captivity of the Israelites at Babylon. Given the fact that this "Babylonian captivity" was followed by the disastrous outbreak of the Great Schism, and that, in turn, by a restoration of papal fortunes bought at the price of abandoning hope of meaningful reform, it is really not too surprising that there has been a strong temptation for historians to portray the whole history of the later medieval Church as a series of interrelated developments leading up inexorably to the final onset of the Protestant Reformation. As one Victorian historian put it, "From Avignon to Constance, from Constance to Basle, from Basle to Luther at the Diet of Worms, we trace an ever-widening path at the end of which appears the Reformation." One simply embarked on the tides of destiny, it seems, at Anagni, to be swept forward with irreversible momentum over seas scattered with the wreckage of thirteenth-century hierocratic ambitions, and to arrive at one's destination, on October 31, 1517, with the banging of Luther's hammer ringing in one's ears.

If this approach has its merits it also has its concomitant drawbacks. By subordinating the complexities of the fourteenth and fifteenth centuries to the rigorous and alien logic of a later era, it introduces order and clarity into a period of notorious confusion. But it does so at the price of simplification and distortion. In lumping together movements as disparate as the Wycliffite, the Hussite and the Conciliarist, it follows the Conciliarists of Constance in their mistaken judgment that Hus's ecclesiology was identical with that of Wyclif, but ignores their further judgment that that ecclesiology was heretical and that Hus, therefore, should be put to death. It has made it possible, as a result, for Protestant historians to portray the whole Conciliar movement as a revolution *manqué,* or, at best, as a *praeparatio evangelica,* and has encouraged their Catholic counterparts to characterize it, with ill-disguised relief, as a revolutionary episode in the life of

34

the Church, something to be handled, in these happier times of ecclesiological normalcy, in an appropriately gingerly fashion.[2]

Again, while serving to emphasize that the deplorable conditions of the "Babylonian captivity" were directly relevant to the outbreak of the Great Schism later on, this approach to the history of the era has served also to overemphasize that fact, to divert attention from the more ancient and fundamental disabilities under which the medieval Church had labored long before the humiliation of Boniface VIII and in the absence of which the more scandalous aspects of the Avignonese era would have been inconceivable. For the roots of the Great Schism and of the Conciliarist crisis were not grounded simply in the unsolved problems of the fourteenth-century ecclesiastical life but were thrust deep into the life of the medieval Church.

Of the numerous weaknesses and disabilities characteristic of that Church, two stand out as being of fundamental importance. They do so because they established the mental categories in terms of which even the most intelligent and spiritually minded men did their thinking on matters ecclesiastical; they do so, also, because they served to set the limits within which even the most zealous and dedicated of Church leaders were forced to maneuver. The first of these disabilities is the politicization of the Church and of the categories of its structural self-understanding.

It is nowadays becoming almost a commonplace to insist that while "in addition to ministries of preaching there are also ministries of welfare and guidance" even in the charismatic communities which Paul describes, there is certainly in those same communities "no ruling class with absolute power and authority".[3] Beyond that, it is also becoming commonplace to acknowledge that when the New Testament authors describe ecclesiastical offices or ministries, they studiously avoid the seemingly obvious

2. See below, ch. 4, pp. 121 ff.
3. Hans Küng, *The Church,* trans. Ray and Rosaleen Ockenden (New York, 1968), p. 398.

words available to them in the Greek vocabulary of politics and choose instead to develop a new term—*diakonia,* service. And their reason for so doing seems to have been this: that whereas the other words available to them expressed "a relationship of rulers and ruled" and carried "overtones of authority, officialdom, rule, dignity or power", this word did not. Bringing with it, instead, connotations of self-abasement, and used by the New Testament authors to denote service to one's fellow men, it is a conception of ecclesiastical office as ministerial, as grounded in love for others, a conception which contrasted sharply with secular notions of office as grounded in power and in law.[4]

As the Christian communities grew in number, size and importance, it is understandable that there should have developed also a tendency to assimilate the biblical notion of office to the less demanding, more familiar, administratively manageable political pattern of thought. But this should not lead one to underestimate the impact upon the Church of the "Constantinian revolution" or of the later disintegration of Roman imperial power. Even before the grant of toleration to Christians in 313, bishops had been acting as legislators, administrators and arbitrators in their churches, but they had been doing so as leaders of private societies, the membership of which was voluntary, leaders whose decisions drew their binding force, therefore, solely from the consciences of the faithful. By the fifth century, however, with the transformation of Christianity from the proscribed creed of a minority to the official civic religion of the Empire, ecclesiastical authority, supported increasingly by the public force of the imperial administration, was becoming coercive in nature and was beginning to reach out into areas which we today would regard as pertaining to the state. These developments persisted during the centuries which followed, and as membership of the Church and membership of the state gradually became coterminous, the distinction between the spiritual and temporal became blurred.

4. Küng, *The Church,* pp. 388-393.

36

There emerged, as a result, a single public society—Church, Christian commonwealth, call it what you will—which was neither voluntary nor private and for the supreme authority over which emperors and popes were later to squabble.

But we are not concerned here with the fact that medieval popes were betrayed by the very dynamic of these politico-ecclesiastical developments into asserting claims to supreme temporal power. By the time of the Great Schism such high-papalist hopes had already been dashed. What concerns us here is the effect of these developments on the original notion of office in the Church. And the major effect was the displacement of the New Testament terminology by an essentially political vocabulary drawn largely from the Roman Law, and the concomitant corrosion of the New Testament understanding of the ministry by a vision of very alien provenance. Thus the word *"jurisdictio"* was taken into canonistic usage from the Roman law at the end of the sixth century (by Gregory the Great, it seems) and used to denote the general administrative activity of ecclesiastical government. By the thirteenth century, with the great revival of legal studies in Europe, canon lawyers were busy distinguishing the ecclesiastical power of jurisdiction (*potestas jurisdictionis*) from the power of orders which priests possessed in virtue of their reception of the sacrament of orders (*potestas ordinis*). That power of jurisdiction, in turn, they saw as a two-fold one in that it was exercised over both the internal and the external forum. The former (*potestas jurisdictionis in foro interiori*) concerned the domain of the individual conscience; it was a power exercised above all by sacramental penance, it was exercised only over those who voluntarily submitted themselves to its sway, and it was directed to the private good. This was not the case, however, with the former, the power of jurisdiction in the public sphere (*potestas jurisdictionis in foro exteriori*), for that was a coercive power pertaining to a public authority, exercised even over the unwilling, and directed to the common good of the faithful. It

37

was, then, a truly governmental power, and to an analysis of this governmental power the canonists devoted much of their attention.[5] By the fourteenth century, with the decline of universal empire and the rise of national monarchies, it was becoming common to distinguish the international Church from the secular states within the boundaries of which it functioned, to treat it as a separate entity, juridically self-sufficient and autonomous. It was to this entity, now, that the term "Christian commonwealth" was attached—and along with it the related terms "ecclesiastical commonwealth", "ecclesiastical polity", "ecclesiastical kingdom" and so on. So that the Church had come to regard itself as a "perfect society", a kingdom over which, by means of a vast bureaucracy, there presided a papal monarch in whom reposed, the canonists commonly argued, the plenitude of jurisdictional power.[6]

By the time of the Avignonese papacy, then, the Church itself had been politicized to a remarkable degree, and, with it, necessarily, the whole notion of office in the Church. Moreover, a second development had occurred which effected a further cor-

5. The history and meaning of these distinctions is analyzed in *Dictionnaire de droit canonique*, VII, s.v. "Pouvoirs de l'église," pp. 71-108. In the last century or so, some canonists have come to regard the magisterial authority as something distinct from jurisdiction: see *Dict. de droit can.*, VI, pp. 695-696, s.v. "Magistère ecclésiastique." Not all, however, agree. Others would argue that because its rulings are obligatory in nature the magisterial authority must indeed be regarded as pertaining to the jurisdictional power. Thus R. J. Banks, *New Catholic Encyclopedia*, VII, s.v. "Jurisdiction (Canon Law)," p. 61: "The common canonical opinion is that the obligatory nature of the Church's teaching constitutes a clear proof that the magisterial power is a part of the Church's jurisdictional authority."

6. A dramatic illustration of this development may be seen in the history of the expression *"corpus Christi mysticum."* By the Conciliar epoch, the doctrine of the Mystical Body had been almost completely secularized, losing its sacramental connotations and acquiring, instead, political and corporational associations—so that, for example, Gerson could speak "with some regularity about the *corpus mysticum* of France." —Ernst H. Kantorowicz, *The King's Two Bodies: A Study in Medieval Political Theology* (Princeton, 1957), pp. 218-219. For this whole issue, see Henri de Lubac, *Corpus Mysticum: l'Eucharistie et l'Eglise au Moyen Age* (Paris, 1944), esp. ch. 5, pp. 117-137.

ruption of that notion and which constituted the second major disability afflicting the medieval Church. That development, an extremely complex one dating back to the barbarian invasions and the impact upon ecclesiastical life both of barbarian custom and feudal institutions, involved the blurring of the crucial distinction which the Romans had made and which we ourselves make between the holding of office and the possession of property.[7] This paralleled a comparable development in secular political life and is reflected in the fact that medievals could use a single word *dominium* to denote both proprietary right and governmental authority.[8] It is reflected also in the fact that the canonists classified the body of rules relating to the disposition of ecclesiastical benefices as belonging not to public but to private law—that is, to the branch of law pertaining to the protection of proprietary rights. It is reflected, again, in the persistent tendency of medievals, clergy and laity alike, to regard ecclesiastical office less as a focus of duty than as a source of income or an object of proprietary right.

(b) The Coming of Schism

It is vital to keep these two enduring disabilities in mind when approaching the Avignonese papacy, the outbreak of the Great Schism, and the subsequent demands of the Conciliarists for constitutional change in the Church and for its reform "in head and members".

Some years ago the French historian Georges Mollat pointed

7. Despite its mistaken preoccupation with Germanic origins, the best introduction to this development remains the classic essay of Ulrich Stutz, "The Proprietary Church as an Element of Mediaeval Germanic Ecclesiastical Law," in Geoffrey Barraclough, trans. and ed., *Mediaeval Germany, 911–1250: Essays by German Historians* (2 vols.; Oxford, 1948), II, pp. 35-70.

8. Whereas the Roman lawyers had used the word solely to denote proprietary right, and we ourselves use its derivative "dominion" to denote authority of a governmental type.

out that it had long been customary for historians, basing themselves uncritically on "the malevolent accounts of contemporary chroniclers", to portray an Avignonese papacy—corrupt, extravagant and tyrannical—as "the source of the greatest evils for the Church and, in the last analysis, the chief cause of the great schism of the West".[9] But, as he also pointed out, the systematic investigation made possible when Leo XIII opened the Vatican archives to scholars had compelled a revision of that estimate, a revision which, while not wholly exonerating the Avignonese pontiffs from the accusations levied against them, had done much to mitigate the sentence usually passed on them. The corruptions and extravagances of the papal court at Avignon, however real, were neither as extensive nor as dramatic as later publicists would have us believe, and it seems to some degree at least that they were reading back into the Avignonese era the confusion, corruption and disastrous financial expediences that characterized the badly shaken papal administration during the years of schism.

And if the schism cannot simply be regarded as the consequence of Avignonese papal policy, neither should it be regarded as the outcome of the Francophilia of the Avignonese pontiffs. Had that been the case, the King of France, in 1378, would presumably not have hesitated, as he did, to lend his support to the cardinals when they disavowed their earlier election of an Italian pontiff and proceeded to the election of the French pope who was later to take up his residence at Avignon. But, then, Mollat established that, French though they and the majority of their cardinals were, the Avignonese popes were by no means consistently or even persistently pro-French in their policies. If national hostilities and alignments undoubtedly helped to protract the schism, they cannot simply be said to have caused it.

Far more important than these factors was the degree to which the policy of the Avignonese pontiffs, several of them very capa-

9. I quote from the English translation of the ninth edition of Georges Mollat, *The Popes at Avignon* (New York, 1963), pp. xiii and 343.

ble men, was simply a further extension of the logic inherent in the thoroughgoing politicization which had already occurred in the Church. Perhaps the most striking feature of that policy was the impetus it gave to the centralization of ecclesiastical administration in the hands of the Roman curia. This process, which had been accelerating for more than a century, was very similar to contemporaneous developments taking place in the national monarchies of Europe, and it was an understandable policy to pursue for men who thought of themselves as monarchs of an ecclesiastical kingdom and possessed of the fullness of jurisictional power in that kingdom. Because of the increasing subservience of the provincial churches to corrupting aristocratic influences, historians are nowadays prone to insist that there was a good deal to be said for such a policy of orderly and coherent centralization. This is perfectly true. At the same time, however, we should not overlook the fact that that policy created its own problems and spawned its own corruptions. Notable among these were the financial system it demanded, the encouragement it gave to the oligarchic aspirations of the cardinals of the Roman *curia,* and the extent to which it provoked a reaction among the provincial churches, driving them away from the bankrupting "protection" of Rome and into the arms of monarchs and princes whose ecclesiastical policies were rarely motivated by truly religious considerations.[10]

Increasing centralization necessitated, understandably, a steady growth in the size of the curial bureaucracy. But how was this to be financed? Loss of control over the papal states in Italy had resulted in a catastrophic decrease in revenue, and if the vigorous prosecution of a series of military compaigns was eventually to recover and pacify those states (thus making possible the return of the papacy to Rome),[11] those campaigns themselves had to be subsidized. As a result, the Avignonese popes involved them-

10. The effects of this reaction were to become evident in the attempts of the fathers at the Council of Basel to remove from papal control matters pertaining to the day-to-day government of the Church.

11. See Mollat, *Popes at Avignon,* pp. 329 ff.

selves in some deplorable financial expedients—above all, in a great extension of the system of "papal provisions" or papal appointment to vacant benefices all over Europe of candidates selected at Rome. Those benefices were regarded and handled, in characteristically medieval (and, as we have seen, perfectly legal) fashion, fundamentally as sources of much needed revenue. The result? The standard abuses of pluralism and non-residence against which so many medieval Church reformers railed. Many prominent ecclesiastical bureaucrats, for example, required by their positions to reside at Rome, amassed in their hands in lieu of salaries whole series of benefices scattered all over Europe, benefices which they would never even visit. And prominent among these ecclesiastics were the cardinals of the Roman *curia* and their numerous protegés.

The centralizing drive of the Avignonese pontiffs had both reflected and enhanced their own claim to possess the plenitude of jurisdictional power in the universal Church. But it had also redounded to the benefit of their most intimate advisers and collaborators, the Roman cardinals whose involvement in the government of the Church had been deepening ever since the eleventh century, when the election of popes had become their prerogative. By the beginning of the fourteenth century their power was already formidable, their financial strength impressive, the perquisites attached to their position multitudinous.[12] Conditions at Avignon encouraged them not only to insist increasingly upon what they considered to be their rightful share in the spoils accruing from papal financial policy (notably from the extension of the system of papal provisions), but also to strengthen their determination to transform into a constitutional right their customary involvement in the making of papal policy. If the papal conception of the shape of Church government was

12. In 1289, for example, Pope Nicholas IV had apportioned to the cardinals no less than half of the revenues which the Roman Church possessed at that time—see W. E. Lunt, *Papal Revenues in the Middle Ages* (New York, 1936), I, pp. 26-27.

unquestionably monarchic, theirs, then, was becoming increasingly oligarchic. Tensions mounted accordingly. "So long as policy, aims and interests of pope and cardinals were identical," Walter Ullmann has said, "there was no reason for resistance on the part of the latter." [13] But once they diverged, trouble was to be expected.

In 1378 they did diverge, in the wake of the first papal election since the return of the papacy to Rome. But the trouble which, as expected, ensued attained unexpectedly serious proportions—nothing less, in fact, than the outbreak of what has since come to be known as the Great Schism of the West.

(c) The Disputed Election of 1378 and Its Aftermath

The story of the events of 1378 is simple enough in its main outlines. In its details, however, it is appallingly complex and hotly disputed. Unfortunately enough, it is the details that proved to be determinative at the time.

It was in 1377 that Gregory XI had finally been persuaded to bring the papacy back to Rome. He did so despite the threat to his life posed by the hostility of the Roman nobles, and by the time of his death in March 1378, he had repented of his decision and had decided to return, once more, to Avignon. After his death the Roman populace was gripped by the fear that such a move might still indeed take place; as a result, the conditions under which the papal election took place were far from ideal. Of the sixteen cardinals who were present for the election, one was Spanish, four were Italian and no less than eleven were French. But the French were divided among themselves, and when the election took place in April it was to the accompaniment, not only of rioting outside the conclave, but also of suspicion and

13. *Origins of the Great Schism* (London, 1949), p. 7. This is the most recent account in English.

dissension within. It ended very quickly, amid scenes of considerable confusion, with the choice of the Archbishop of Bari, a compromise candidate who took the title of Urban VI. The Roman mob had clamored noisily for the election of a Roman. The cardinals, unwilling to accede to this demand but divided among themselves and (they were later to claim) in fear of their lives, had been forced for the first time in over half a century to choose a non-French pope. The Archbishop of Bari was not a Roman, but he enjoyed the twin advantages of being an Italian, and, at the same time, a curial official who had served long and faithfully at Avignon. While the fact of his nationality might appease the Romans, it seemed reasonable to expect that he would also be subservient to the wishes of the cardinals. His subsequent behavior, however, did not vindicate such hopes, and his treatment of the cardinals—violent, erratic, abusive, suggestive even of insanity—led to a rapid worsening of relations with them. In May and June of 1378 all the cardinals with the exception of the four Italians left Rome and made their way to Anagni where they would be outside the area subject to papal control. There, in August, they publicly denounced Urban's election as made under duress and as a result invalid. Finally, in September, joined now by the three surviving Italian cardinals,[14] they proceeded to elect Robert of Geneva, one of themselves, in his place. He assumed the title of Clement VII and, shortly thereafter, took up residence at Avignon.

Since neither of the rival claimants proved to be able to displace the other or to command the allegiance of all the Christian nations, the schism thus engendered was of a far more serious nature than its numerous predecessors in the West had been. Despite all efforts by churchmen and temporal rulers to end it, it was to endure for almost forty years. Both claimants went on to appoint whole new batches of cardinals; both obdurately refused, either individually or concurrently, to withdraw. Loyalties

14. The fourth had died on September 7. Thus Clement VII was elected by all surviving electors of Urban VI.

quickly hardened, and, as the years went by, their rival curias strove to perpetuate their claims. Benedict XIII was elected at Avignon to succeed Clement VII, and Boniface IX, Innocent VII and Gregory XII, in turn, to succeed Urban VI at Rome. The result: the development of an exceedingly grave constitutional crisis within the Church.

It has been customary to place much of the blame for this development on the national animosities then prevailing in Europe, and also on the pretensions and ambitions of the cardinals. There is much to be said for this point of view. The territorial composition of the two papal "obediences", Roman and Avignonese, is entirely predictable in terms of previous political and diplomatic alignments. Again, the resentment which the cardinals betrayed at Urban's ill-tempered assaults upon their dignity, their privileges and their opulent style of life is well-attested. Nevertheless, recent studies of the disputed election and of its background converge on the conclusion that the doubts which the cardinals later expressed about the validity of Urban's title have to be taken more seriously than has, in the past, been usual.[15] The uncertainty caused by the violence outside the conclave and the fear within was admitted at the time. Those who argued, then and later, for the validity of Urban's election, based their case, not on the facts of the election itself, but on the subsequent behavior of the cardinals—their participation in his coronation, their performance of homage to him, their delay in challenging the validity of his election, and so on. Current research, however, has emphasized the degree to which their behavior at Rome in the weeks following the election was the result of coercion and fear and fell short, therefore, of "full and free consent". It has

15. See K. A. Fink, "Zur Beurteilung des Grossen Abendländischen Schismas," *Zeitschrift für Kirchengeschichte* LXXIII (1962), 337-339, and the works referred to therein, notably M. Seidlmayer, *Die Anfänge des Grossen Abendländischen Schismas* (Münster, 1940), and O. Prerovsky, *L'elezione di Urbano VI et l'insorgere dello scisma d'Occidente.* Ullmann's account in his *Origins* marks something of an exception to this trend. Cf. August Franzen, "The Council of Constance: Present State of the Problem," *Concilium*, VII, 34 ff.

emphasized, too, their real doubts about the sanity of the new pope and the extent to which such doubts were justifiable.[16]

This being the case, however real their other motives, the cardinals clearly had some valid grounds for questioning the legitimacy of Urban's claim to be pope. Similarly, however convenient it may have been to their own political interests, those rulers who aligned themselves with Clement VII (sometimes, it should be noted, after considerable hesitation) were able to do so with good conscience. Again, however desirable a clear solution to this vexing problem may be, the historical evidence simply does not permit one the anachronism of imposing a dogmatic solution and insisting on the exclusive legitimacy of Urban VI's title to the papacy, and, therefore, of the titles of his successors in the Roman line. Though this has often been done,[17] and especially at Rome, it should be remembered that it was not the Urbanists alone who had the support of dedicated Christians, lay and clerical. If a St. Catherine of Siena supported Urban, a St. Vincent Ferrer supported Clement. Men at the time, it seems, were in a state of "invincible ignorance" and *a fortiori* so, too, are we. The best we can do is to recognize the fact that after April 8, 1378, there was one man with a doubtful claim to the papacy, and, after September 20, 1378, two.

(d) The Council of Pisa (1409)

The thirty years which followed witnessed numerous attempts to bring the schism to an end. Hope centered initially on the possibility of successful arbitration between the two claimants and still more on the possibility of convoking a general council representing the entire Church to render a judgment on the re-

16. Later on, the cardinals of his own creation were so convinced of Urban's incapacity as to toy with the idea of subjecting him to the control of a council of guardianship, an idea for which several of them paid dearly when Urban discovered this "plot" against him and had them imprisoned and tortured. See Ullmann, *Origins*, pp. 167-168.

17. See below, ch. 4, pp. 111 ff., 121 ff.

spective validity of the two contested elections. This latter view was given forceful expression in 1379–81 by the German theologians Conrad of Gelnhausen and Henry of Langenstein. The "Conciliar movement" was something of a reality, then, right from the beginning of the schism.

As time went on, however, and as members of both obediences began to regard both claimants as sharing equally the responsibility for protracting the schism, support shifted to what was known as the *via cessionis,* a plan which envisaged the renunciation of their claims by the rival pontiffs and the subsequent combination of the two colleges of cardinals to elect a new and universally accepted pope. This was particularly true in the years after 1394 when the cardinals at Avignon, on the death of Clement VII, ignored the pleas of the French king and insisted on proceeding to the election of a new pope. These were years of mounting pressure on behalf of the *via cessionis,* pressure applied on the Roman pope by the German emperor and on his Avignonese rival by the French king—the latter going so far in his attempts to coerce an abdication as to embark in 1398 on a unilateral national withdrawal of obedience from the pope.

This failed, as did all subsequent efforts to promote the *via cessionis,* but the years of barren diplomacy bore unexpected fruit towards the end of 1408 in the revival once more of the idea of resorting to a general council. This became a feasible alternative when the collapse of a final round of negotiations between the Roman and Avignonese popes led disgusted cardinals from both camps to forswear allegiance to their respective pontiffs. Gathering together at Leghorn and addressing themselves to the secular rulers and bishops of both obediences, they summoned a general council of the whole Church to meet in Italy. When this action drew widespread support, the rival pontiffs in desperation summoned their own councils. But both of these papal councils were very poorly attended and neither could boast of the impressively ecumenical character of the council which opened at Pisa on March 28, 1409.

This council of Pisa enjoyed the support of the greater part of Christendom. It was attended by four patriarchs, 24 cardinals, about 100 bishops (with another hundred or so represented by proxies), 107 abbots (180 more sent their proctors), the generals of the mendicant orders and of most other religious orders, about 700 theologians and canonists, and representatives of 13 universities, of many cathedral chapters and of most European princes. When the two rival pontiffs refused to cooperate with it, the assembly declared itself to be canonically constituted and an ecumenical council and then embarked upon a careful legal process directed against the two popes. It culminated on June 9, 1409, with their formal deposition as schismatics and heretics.

In so doing, the council fathers followed the generally accepted canonistic teaching of the day that a pope who deviated from the true faith or who was guilty of notorious crimes which scandalized the Church and were, therefore, tantamount to heresy was liable to judgment by the Church and even to deposition. In so doing, they also followed a widespread and well-established canonistic opinion to the effect that, while in such a legal process the cardinals had certain powers of initiative, the body competent to proceed to judgment was the general council.[18] Certainly, the greater part of Christendom seems to have regarded their action as valid, as also their election on June 26 of a new pope, Alexander V. The Roman and Avignonese pontiffs were left with drastically reduced obediences and their survival may have been assured only by the death of Alexander V in 1410 and the succession of John XXIII, a man of evil and notorious life. For, as one recent scholar has concluded, "if the popes of Pisa were afterward considered anti-popes, the reason seems to be that the second Pope of Pisa, John XXIII, showed such unworthy behavior that he dragged his predecessor and the whole Council of Pisa with him in his own catastrophic fall."[19]

18. See below, ch. 3, pp. 80 ff.
19. A. Brüggen, "Die Predigten des Pisaner Konzils" (unpublished dissertation; Freiburg, 1963), 129; cited in Franzen, "Council of Constance," 42.

(e) The Council of Constance (1414-18)

But whatever the might-have-beens of history, what actually emerged from the Council of Pisa was in fact the addition of a third line of claimants to the Roman and Avignonese lines already existing—a clearly intolerable situation which led, in 1413, to the summoning of the Council of Constance, itself so well attended that it has often been described as "the greatest representative assembly of the whole Middle Ages".[20]

John XXIII himself convoked the council but he did so with extreme reluctance and only under pressure from the Emperor-elect Sigismund, who was to play a prominent role throughout the conciliar proceedings. For John, the council was to be a continuation of the Council of Pisa, and he hoped with the support of the multitudinous Italian bishops to secure another condemnation of his rivals and renewed confirmation of his own papal title. Those hopes were dashed, however, when the northern Europeans within a few months of the opening of the council in November 1414 insisted that voting be by conciliar "nations"—eventually five in all—each one of them casting a single vote in the general conciliar sessions irrespective of the number of its members.[21] The council then proceeded, early in

20. In his *Chronicle of the Council of Constance,* the contemporary writer Ulrich Richental, who had a taste for statistics, listed as being in attendance, in addition to Popes John XXIII and Martin V and a host of other officials, temporal and spiritual, 5 patriarchs, 33 cardinals, 47 archbishops, 145 bishops, 93 suffragan bishops, 132 abbots, 155 priors, 217 doctors of theology, 361 doctors of both laws, 5,300 "simple priests and scholars", over 3,000 merchants, shopkeepers, craftsmen, musicians and players, and over 700 "harlots in brothels"—these last to be distinguished from those "who lay in stables and wherever they could, beside the private ones whom I could not count". Translation in J. H. Mundy and K. M. Woody, eds., *The Council of Constance* (London and New York, 1961), p. 182.

21. These "nations", like the nations of the medieval universities were, in fact, combinations of nationalities. Thus, the "English" nation included the Irish and Scottish, the German included Poles, Czechs, Scandinavians and others. All debate took place in the separate meetings of the nations and in

1415, to take up the problem of the schism, and, in so doing, was led inevitably to focus its attention on the notorieties of John XXIII's life.

Over the course of the next three years until its dissolution in April 1418 it was to embark on many projects and it was to take some very important actions—notably the condemnation of the teachings of Wyclif and Hus, the condemnation of tyrannicide and the promulgation of a series of reform measures.[22] But none of these conciliar achievements can vie in importance with the successful termination of the schism and the election of a pope the validity of whose title was accepted by the whole Church. And it is these remarkable developments that concern us here.

Faced by the threat of a public investigation of his alleged crimes, John XXIII played for time by promising to resign his office. At the same time he planned in secret to flee from the council, to disrupt thereby its activities, and perhaps even to wreck it. His plan very nearly succeeded. His flight to Schaff-hausen on March 20, 1415, caused great alarm and confusion among the council fathers. Had not Sigismund rallied them, the assembly, in the absence of the pope who had convoked it, might well have disintegrated. But as it became clear that John was unlikely to return and was probably planning to go back on his solemn pledge to resign, the determination of the fathers to proceed was strengthened and their sentiments became increasingly conciliarist. As a result, at the fifth general session, the council formally promulgated the decree *Haec sancta,* declaring that the Council of Constance was a lawful general council, that it derived its authority immediately from Christ, and that all

___

a special "steering committee" which was made up of representatives from each nation. From July 1415 onwards, the College of Cardinals, as a corporate body comparable to the nations, was permitted to cast a single vote in the general sessions of the council.

22. A rather weak and disappointing series, the most significant measure being the decree *Frequens* (October 5, 1417), by the terms of which general councils, after the ending of Constance, were to assemble at frequent and ultimately regular intervals.

Christians, including the pope himself, were bound to obey it on pain of punishment in matters pertaining to the faith, the ending of the schism and the reform of the Church.[23] This decree has been a controversial one but there can be no doubt that the subsequent activity of the council was grounded in the claims it advanced.

On May 17, 1415, John XXIII was taken prisoner. On May 29 he was deposed—not, it should be noted, because the council questioned the legitimacy of his title, but because it had tried him and found him guilty of simony, perjury and other forms of scandalous misconduct. This sentence he did not challenge. Less than two months later, Gregory XII, the Roman pope, offered to resign provided only that he were permitted himself to convoke the council, thus legitimating it in his own eyes and in the eyes of his followers. By so doing, of course, he could also claim to have received from the council at least tacit confirmation of the legitimacy of the Roman line of popes. The council fathers were not unaware of this, but their overriding objective was unity, they had his promise to resign, and they were even less disposed to make a fuss about a formality, which very few of them took seriously, than they had been in the previous year to treat the ambassadors of *both* Gregory XII and Benedict XIII as official papal delegates rather than merely as private Christians—and this despite the fact that they themselves had recognized John XXIII as legitimate pope.

Accordingly, on July 4, 1415, Gregory's bull of convocation was read to the council and his abdication then accepted. His Avignonese rival did not give in so easily, and, surrounded by a tiny coterie of adamant supporters, persisted in his claim to be the one true pope until his death in 1423. But, by then, events had passed him by. On July 26, 1417, long after the members of his

---

23. Often known, though improperly, as *Sacrosancta,* the title of the similar decree promulgated at Basel in 1439. A translation of the text appears below, ch. 2, pp. 75-76.

obedience had deserted him and declared their adhesion to the
council, he was judged guilty of "perjury, heresy and schism"
and declared deposed. Less than a year later an enlarged body of
electors, including deputies from each conciliar nation as well as
the cardinals of all three obediences, went into conclave to
choose a new pope. And with the election on November 11, 1417,
of one of the cardinals of the Roman obedience who had adhered
to the Council of Pisa and who now took the title of Martin V,
the years of doubt were over, the Church had at last an unquestionably legitimate pope, and the Great Schism was at an end.

(f) The Council of Basel-Ferrara-Florence (1431-49)

But if the schism was ended, the "Conciliar movement" was not.
For if the schism was ended, it was only because a general council had formally claimed supreme power in the Church on certain
crucial matters, had been willing, further, to enforce that claim,
and, in the decree *Frequens,* had been careful enough to set up
constitutional machinery to impede any reversion to papal absolutism. This machinery proved to be less effective than doubtless
they had hoped, but clearly not as ineffective as Martin V seems
to have wished. In accordance with the provisions of *Frequens,*
Martin in 1423 summoned a new council to meet at Pavia. He
transferred it to Siena and, then, because it was very poorly
attended, dissolved it. Seven years later, again in accordance with
Frequens, but this time only under pressure, he convoked another
council to meet at Basel. Shortly thereafter he died. When the
council opened it did so under his successor Eugenius IV, a much
less decisive man, and under somewhat discouraging circumstances.

Two great external issues were to do much to determine its
fate: the Hussite wars and the quest for reunion with the Greek
orthodox. The "great matter" of the council was still, neverthe-

less, the constitutional question of the relationship of pope to general council. One might have assumed that this had been settled at Constance—both by the theoretical pronouncements of the council and by the action it had taken. But its failure to achieve any really thoroughgoing reform of the Church and especially of the papal administration, the inability or unwillingness of Martin V himself to implement such a reform on his own authority, his ambivalence and that of his successor towards the Conciliarist constitutional claims, and their attitude of "business as usual" when it came to operating the central administrative machinery of the Church—all of these factors helped sponsor among the ecclesiastics assembled at Basel a deep suspicion and fear of papal intentions. They helped sponsor, too, a violent reaction against the papal claims to plenitude of power and against the centralized mechanisms of papal administration as these had developed over the last two centuries and more.

It was Eugenius himself who precipitated the crisis. When the council opened on July 23, 1431, there was not a single bishop present and attendance remained very sparse up to the month of October.[24] Because Martin V had reached an agreement with the Greeks to hold a council of reunion on Italian soil, Eugenius was anxious not to prolong the life of what seemed already to be a moribund assembly. On December 18, therefore, he proceeded to dissolve the Council of Basel. But he had misjudged the mood of the council fathers. He had also misjudged the priorities of Cardinal Cesarini, the man he himself had deputed as legate to preside over the council. In the wake of a crusade against the Hussites which had met with disastrous defeat, Cesarini had committed Basel to vital negotiations with the moderate party of the

24. The number of bishops in attendance at Basel never became very impressive. "In a vote taken on December 5, 1436, three cardinals, nineteen bishops and twenty-nine abbots were faced by three hundred and three other participants at the council: the bishops, therefore, formed much less than a tenth of the participants." Hubert Jedin, *Ecumenical Councils of the Catholic Church,* trans. Ernest Graf (London and New York, 1960), p. 129.

victors. These negotiations were now threatened by the papal bull of dissolution. When it arrived, therefore, he joined with the council fathers in refusing to obey the pope. Deadlock ensued, and, as support for the pope dwindled and as men of the stature of Cesarini and Nicholas of Cusa rallied to its support, the council proceeded to reaffirm Conciliar principles and to put them into practice.

In 1432 it republished the bull *Haec sancta,* and, in the years which followed, it devoted its energies not only to the struggle with the pope, but also to the negotiation of a Hussite settlement and to reform of the Church in "head and members". It was the conclusion of an agreement with the Hussites that finally brought the pope to heel. That settlement was greeted with great relief in Germany and eastern Europe, enhancing the council's prestige and making the pope's opposition to its activities well-nigh indefensible. In December 1433, therefore, he capitulated. In the bull *Dudum sacrum* he declared his earlier dissolution of the council invalid and proclaimed that its conciliar activity was, and had been, legitimate all along. The following June, at its eighteenth general session, the council, flushed with victory, solemnly reaffirmed *Haec sancta.*

It must have seemed at the time that the victory of the Conciliarists was complete. But their own conception of what constituted meaningful reform in the Church proved to be their undoing. If they managed to take one or two steps to promote reform of the lower clergy, and if they discussed a good many more, the bulk of their effort was directed, nevertheless, to reform of "head" rather than of "members". And that reform was concerned mainly with the curtailing of papal financial resources and the limiting of papal administrative powers. Against such measures Eugenius protested in vain. It was not until 1437 that he was able to impose his will, and then only because the council by its actions had begun to forfeit the support of some of its most distinguished adherents. By that time "the representatives of the lower clergy, the chapters and the universities, and the

54

horde of doctors, had long ago gained an overwhelming ascendancy at Basle, while the bishops were withdrawing from a Council which, after creating a curia of its own, was deeply engaged in the business of allocating prebends".[25] As a result, when, on September 18, 1437, Eugenius transferred the council to Ferrara, which the Greeks had accepted as the site for the council of union, a significant minority of the council membership—including Cesarini, Nicholas of Cusa and other luminaries—obeyed the decree.

The majority, it is true, remained at Basel where it went on to proclaim the superiority of council over pope to be an undeniable article of faith, to declare Eugenius IV deposed as a heretic, and to elect in his place Duke Amadeus of Savoy. He took the title of Felix V, won support in Switzerland and Austria and from several universities, and benefited from the declared neutrality of France and Germany. Nevertheless, it was a blunder on behalf of the Basel rump-council thus to have precipitated a new schism within the Latin church, especially when the papal council of Ferrara-Florence had just succeeded in ending the ancient schism between Greeks and Latins. Both of these events, certainly, worked to ensure the final victory of Eugenius IV. The deepening radicalism of the Conciliarists did little to bolster their flagging fortunes, and on April 7, 1449, after France had followed the example of Germany in renouncing her neutrality and rallying to the side of Eugenius, Felix V resigned. On April 25 the Council of Basel (transferred a year earlier to Lausanne) decreed its own dissolution. With this ignominious ending of Basel, the Conciliar movement is usually regarded as having met its decisive defeat. But this did not mean the extinction of Conciliar theory [26] and it is now time to turn to a detailed examination of that theory.

25. Hubert Jedin, *A History of the Council of Trent,* trans. Ernest Graf (St. Louis), I, p. 19.
26. See below, ch. 3, pp. 85 ff.

CHAPTER 2

The Conciliar Theory Examined

(a) The Early Radicals: Ockham and Marsilius

During the summer of 1378, in their efforts to void the election of Urban VI, the dissident cardinals assembled at Anagni had turned to the French king, Charles V, for help. The first to suggest that recourse be had to a general council for a judgment were either the lawyers to whom Charles V turned for counsel in this delicate situation or the three Italian cardinals, who, at this point, were still seeking on behalf of Urban VI to negotiate a settlement.

These suggestions met with no response, and when the *via concilii* was next advanced, it was in the context of schism and under extraordinary circumstances that called for extraordinary measures. In the works of Conrad of Gelnhausen and Henry of Langenstein, therefore, it took the form of what has come to be known as the Conciliar theory. Indeed, Gelnhausen's *Epistola concordiae* (May 1380) has been described as "a turning point in the history of the Schism" precisely because it was "the first systematic exposition" of that theory.[1] The earlier writers on the history of Conciliarism were content to regard the views expressed in this tract primarily as a response to the grievous difficulties occasioned by the schism. But later historians were to push back beyond the immediate context in which Gelnhausen and Langenstein had framed their views, and to claim to have found an earlier source for Conciliar theory in the great efflorescence

---

1. Walter Ullmann, *The Origins of the Great Schism* (London, 1948), p. 176.

56

of publicistic literature occasioned in the first half of the fourteenth century by the bitter clash between the Avignonese papacy and Lewis of Bavaria. In particular, they claimed to have found that source in the works of the two imperialist publicists, William of Ockham (d. 1349) and Marsilius of Padua (d. *ca.* 1342).

The implications of this attribution should not escape us. In the last great medieval struggle between the supreme spiritual and temporal authorities in Christendom these men had sided with the temporal, and neither have been in good standing with modern Catholic theologians. In Ockham's works it is often difficult to identify amid the complex interplay of opinions adduced and analyzed those views that are truly his own. Even in the case of final positions that are clearly identifiable as his it is often equally difficult to assess their true drift because of the subtle nuances he has introduced during the course of their development.[2] And it is tempting to think that only because of these difficulties did his views escape formal condemnation.

Nevertheless, it would be improper to ignore the fact that there is in Ockham a certain ambivalence that makes it possible to read him in more ways than one. If later Conciliar thinkers could find in his writings a good deal of piecemeal support for their views, we should not overlook the fact that these works contained also some crumbs of hope for their opponents. Thus, on the one hand, his anti-papal critique is extensive and devastating. It is election by the faithful (or those designated by them), he says, that confers on the chosen candidate the position of pope, and the need for their consent serves further to limit the extent of the papal power. The universal Church is nothing other than the

2. Thus, whereas at first he seems tempted to reject the crucial traditional distinction between "power of orders" and "power of jurisdiction" and to deny to the pope anything that could be called a coercive jurisdiction, he maintains neither that rejection nor that denial and is willing finally to admit that the pope possesses by divine right a limited coercive power. For a discussion of this critical point, see Georges de Lagarde, *La naissance de l'esprit laïque au déclin du moyen age* (Paris, 1963), V, pp. 175 ff.

congregation of the faithful; to that universal Church alone, and not to the (local) Roman church, belongs the indefectibility that Christ promised his apostles. The universal Church will never lapse totally into heresy, but as in the past popes have done so, they may well do so again, and, in that event, they are of course subject to judgment. Even though the canon law provides that the pope alone may convoke a general council, equity requires that in the event of papal heresy a council can be assembled by other means, can stand in judgment on the pope, and can have him replaced. Furthermore, because "what touches all ought to be discussed and approved by all", and "since the Church is not the pope or the congregation of the priests but the congregation of the faithful" the elected representatives of the council should include lay people and even women.[3]

Radical enough, no doubt. On the other hand, however, too much has often been made of Ockham's references to the role of the general council, for it is by no means central to his ecclesiology. Indeed, it would be futile to look in his works for "a coherent theory of the rights of a general council".[4] And not without reason. For he is not, according to the usual general understanding of the term, a Conciliarist at all. He does not attribute to the council the supreme jurisdictional power in the Church. If it *can* judge and replace an heretical pope, it is not necessarily his "natural judge", since (at least according to Ockham's final opinion) "a heretical pope was *ipso facto* deposed and so subject to the judgment of any Catholic"—bishop, assembly of bishops, or, even, the Emperor.[5] It is true that general councils represent the universal Church, but, then, representatives do not necessarily enjoy all the prerogatives pertaining to the community represented. The council no more enjoys the prerogative of infallibility than does the pope, whose office, after

3. *Octo quaestiones de Potestate Papae*, q. 1, dist. xvii; ed. J. G. Sykes, *Guillelmi de Ockham Opera Politica* (Manchester, 1940), I, p. 60.

4. De Lagarde, *Naissance*, V, p. 53.

5. Brian Tierney, "Ockham, the Conciliar Theory, and the Canonists," *Journal of the History of Ideas*, XV (1954), 60-61.

all, is of divine origin, who himself represents the Church, and who is normally charged with the task of convoking councils.[6] An heretical pope can doubtless be subjected to the judgment of a council, but it should also be noted that if all the other members of a general council lapsed into heresy and the pope himself did not, then they would all be subject to *his* judgment.[7]

And so on. The complexity of the argumentation is appalling and formidable. It is true that the taint of heresy attached itself to what were thought to be his views, but it would seem that if later Conciliarists drew their ideas from Ockham, they must have done so at the price of distorting and simplifying him. With Marsilius, however, it is a different matter. As evidenced in his great work the *Defensor Pacis* (1324), the thrust of his thinking is vigorous and its direction unmistakable—so much so, indeed, that John XXII lost no time but proceeded formally, as early as 1327, to condemn him as a heretic.

And not without cause. Marsilius's instinct is to go for the jugular of the traditional medieval ecclesiology. Like Ockham, and like others of unimpeachable orthodoxy, he argues that the Church is not to be defined as the clerical body alone but as the "whole body of the faithful who believe in and invoke the name of Christ".[8] But unlike Ockham and unlike those others, Marsilius concludes from this that faith being a voluntary thing the congregation of the faithful must lack the type of coerced unity which is proper to truly political bodies. His church, then, is "a purely spiritual congregation of believers, connected by no ties but their common faith and participation in the sacraments".[9] This being so, there is no room in that church for the exercise by its ministers of any coercive jurisdictional power, any *potestas*

6. *Dialogus,* I, V, xxv; ed., Melchior Goldast, *Monarchia S. Romani Imperii* (Frankfurt, 1614), II, p. 494.
7. *Dialogus,* I, VI, lxiv; Goldast, II, p. 571.
8. *Defensor Pacis,* II, ii, 3; I cite the translation of Alan Gewirth, *Marsilius of Padua: The Defender of Peace* (New York, 1956), II, p. 103. See the useful introductory synopsis in this edition, pp. xix ff.
9. Gewirth, *Marsilius of Padua,* I, p. 277.

jurisdictionis in foro exteriori.[10] Indeed, the traditional division of ecclesiastical authority into power of orders and power of jurisdiction cannot really be sustained, for the latter is the prerogative of the political authority and the political authority alone.

This is not to say, however, that Marsilius refuses to recognize the existence of a divinely established priesthood. He certainly does so, and he is willing to discuss the role of the priest in the administration of the sacraments of penance and holy orders. But his attitude to the latter is revealing. The "bestowal of orders" is a power that pertains not just to bishops but to all priests. The inequalities in the priesthood have no divine basis whatsoever. The Church can have no real head but Christ, its founder. The great hierarchical structure of bishops, archbishops and pope is not of divine provenance at all. It is simply a human contrivance, explicable only in terms of administrative convenience and justifiable only to the extent to which it is grounded in the consent of the faithful. And that consent is to be expressed by direct election of priests, bishops and "head bishop". It is to be expressed, also, by the general council—an elective body composed of laity as well as clergy, the supreme prerogative of which, as the body representative of the faithful, is to be able to express itself on matters of faith with that infallibility which Christ promised neither to Peter or his supposed successors, nor to the apostles or their clerical successors, but to the universal Church alone.

There can be no mistaking the radicalism of this Marsilian ecclesiology. It is heady stuff and its condemnation is perfectly understandable. If it is indeed the source of the later Conciliar theory, then that theory was branded as heterodox right from the start, and its traditional dismissal by Catholic historians and theologians alike as a revolutionary deviation in the history of the medieval Church is wholly comprehensible. But, then, when one turns to the works written by the Conciliar theorists of the "classical era"—the period stretching from the outbreak of the schism to the disintegration of the Council of Basel—the at-

10. See above, ch. 1, p. 37.

tempt to derive their ecclesiology from that of Ockham or Marsilius does not hold up under examination.

Borrowings from Ockham, it is true, there are many, and they extend in the case of the Conciliarist Pierre d'Ailly (1350-1420) to verbatim copyings. These borrowings, however, are piecemeal in nature. If they reflect the willingness of the Conciliarists to cash in on Ockham's destructive critique of the traditional papalist ecclesiology, they reflect also their blindness to the equally destructive effects of that critique when directed at the conciliarist ecclesiology which they themselves wished to promote. Signs of Marsilian influence are much less in evidence. Both Dietrich of Niem (d. 1418) and Nicholas of Cusa drew some material from the *Defensor Pacis,* but the presence even of piecemeal borrowings in the works of most of these Conciliarists is hard to detect, and it would seem that the radicalism of the Marsilian vision was simply too much for them to take.

The roots of the theory propounded by these Conciliarists of the classical era are to be found, then, neither in the immediate circumstances of the Great Schism nor in the writings of their more radical forebears, Ockham and Marsilius. And if one may explain the Ockhamist attribution in terms of the obvious complexity of *his* thinking, the curious allegation of a Marsilian source must surely spring from the less obvious complexity of the Conciliar theory itself and from the frequent misunderstandings to which that complexity has given rise. It is most important, therefore, to be quite clear about the meaning one is to assign to such expressions as "Conciliarism" and "Conciliar theory" and it is now time to attempt such a clarification.

(b) Conciliarism of the Classical Era

Whatever its subsequent incapsulations might suggest, the Conciliar thinking of the classical age betrays many more variations than we tend often to assume—too many, indeed, and too elusive to trap within the framework of any simple classification. It is possible, however, to discern within the pattern of that thinking three broad strands, distinct in their origins, distinct also in their subsequent careers (as we shall see),[11] but woven momentarily and fatefully into a meaningful and historic configuration.

The first of these three strands is the demand for reform of the Church in head and members and the belief that this reform could best be achieved and consolidated through the periodic assembly of general councils. Though official Conciliar ratification was given to this point of view in the decree *Frequens,* promulgated in 1417 at Constance and providing for the assembly of general councils at frequent and regular intervals, this first strand did not *necessarily* involve any assertion of the superiority of council to pope—the element which, as we shall see, was central to another strand, the "strict" Conciliar theory.

The origins of this first strand long predated the schism. By the end of the thirteenth century the call for reform was becoming increasingly insistent. It was directed especially at the papal centralization of authority at Rome and the affiliated systems of papal taxation and provision to benefices. In the early years of the fourteenth century, Guilielmus Durantis (the Younger), in a tract occasioned by the convocation of the Council of Vienne (1311–12), had linked this demand for reform with a proposal that general councils assembled at regular ten-yearly intervals would be an appropriate means for achieving that desirable goal. But he produced no systematic ecclesiology and it would certainly be improper to regard him as a proponent of the strict Conciliar theory. As Jedin has said, "it required the pitiful situation created by the Schism to bring about the alliance of Conciliar theory with the demand for reform."[12] Once that alliance was concluded, however, the destinies of both were interwoven throughout the course of the Conciliar movement.

11. See below, ch. 3, pp. 85 ff.
12. Hubert Jedin, *A History of the Council of Trent,* trans. Ernest Graf (St. Louis, 1957), I, p. 9.

As early as 1381, in advocating the assembly of a general council to end the schism, Henry of Langenstein painted a graphic picture of the prevalence of corruption in the Church, ascribed its persistence to the lack of general councils, and saw reform as one of the major tasks of his projected council of reunion.[13] In so doing, he set the tone of much that was to follow. In 1402-3, for instance, Pierre d'Ailly sketched out a whole plan of reform in his *De materia concilii generalis,* a plan which he was later to present to the fathers of Constance.[14] Again, in his *De Modis Uniendi et reformandi ecclesiae* (1410), Dietrich of Niem assumed that reunion and reform of the Church went hand in hand and that a council was necessary to achieve both.[15] Like d'Ailly he repeated many of these ideas at Constance where, indeed, as later on at Basel, the view most widely shared among council fathers of differing opinions and backgrounds was the conviction that the frequent assembly of general councils was a necessary precondition for any truly effective reform of the Church.

This, then, was the most prominent strand in Conciliarist thinking. The second strand was the least prominent. Nor is this too surprising, given the fact that reform was most persistently conceived as reform of the Roman *curia* and the restriction of its authority over the universal Church. For the second strand envisaged the constitution of the Church in oligarchic terms, its government ordinarily in the hands of the *curia,* the pope being limited in his power by that of the cardinals, with whose "advice,

13. In his *Epistola concilii pacis,* chs. 16-19, in Jean Gerson, *Opera Omnia,* ed. Louis Ellies Dupin (Antwerp, 1706), II, cols. 835-840. (Cited henceforth as Dupin.)

14. See the edition in Francis Oakley, *The Political Thought of Pierre d'Ailly: The Voluntarist Tradition* (New Haven and London, 1964), App. III, pp. 314 ff. The plan is described in a chapter on d'Ailly which I contributed to B. A. Gerrish, ed., *Reformers in Profile* (Philadelphia, 1967), pp. 49 ff.

15. This work has been edited by H. E. Heimpel, *Dietrich von Niem. Dialog über Union and Reform der Kirche, 1410* (Leipzig and Berlin, 1933).

consent, direction and remembrance" he had to rule.[16] This was the point of view which inspired the dissident cardinals in 1378 when they rejected the demand for a general council and took it upon themselves to pass judgment on the validity of Urban VI's election.[17] Those who were not members of the Sacred College and who were already convinced that a general council alone was the proper forum for deciding so important a question were understandably unimpressed. Certainly, we would look in vain for any trace of sympathy with such oligarchic ambitions in the works of Conrad of Gelnhausen and Henry of Langenstein.

Later on, it is true, in describing the Church as a "polity" or "mixed government", Jean Gerson referred to the College of Cardinals as "imitating" the aristocratic power.[18] But he does not develop the idea, and, as one might have expected, it is only among those Conciliarists who were themselves members of the Sacred College that the oligarchic strand is clearly evident. In the years immediately preceding Constance it was advocated with great clarity by Franciscus Zabarella, the most distinguished canonist of the day; at Constance itself Pierre d'Ailly defended it; [19] among the Conciliarists of Basel, Nicholas of Cusa indicated his own sympathy with it.

We have already seen [20] that this oligarchic vision of the ecclesiastical constitution was rooted in traditional curial claims based on the de facto share increasingly taken by the cardinals

16. The words are taken from the alleged *professio fidei* of Boniface VIII. See S. Baluzius and J. Mansi, *Miscellenea* (Lucae, 1761-64), III, p. 418. They are cited by d'Ailly in his *Tractatus de ecclesiastica potestate,* Dupin, II, cols. 929-930.

17. It was this same point of view which helps to explain the behavior of some of the cardinals later on at the Council of Constance. These cardinals, while they refused to follow John XXIII in his flight from the council, balked nevertheless at the council's own claim that it was superior in authority to the Roman See.

18. *De potestate ecclesiastica,* Dupin, II, col. 254.

19. In so doing, he manifested his own increasing preoccupation with the dignity and importance of the cardinalate in the years after 1411 when he himself became a cardinal; see Oakley, *Political Thought of Pierre d'Ailly,* p. 119, n. 20.

20. See above, ch. 1, pp. 42-43.

in the day to day government of the universal Church. These traditional claims received what seems to have been their first theoretical formulation in an anonymous commentary on the *Decretum* of Gratian (the first book of the medieval *corpus* of canon law) written early in the thirteenth century. This formulation was given more explicit expression by the later canonists Hostiensis (d. 1271) and Johannes Monachus (d. 1313), who maintained that the cardinals shared with the pope the exercise of the "fullness of power" (*plenitudo potestatis*). But all of these men took as their premiss the idea that "Pope and Cardinals together formed a single corporate body subject to the normal rules of corporation law," so that "the Pope stood in exactly the same relationship to the Cardinals as any other Bishop to his cathedral chapter." [21] And, for them, it should be noted, "authority in a corporation was not concentrated in the head alone but resided in all the members; and . . . the prelate could not act without consent of the members in the more important matters affecting the well-being of the whole corporation." [22] In the decision-making process, then, the cardinals were to have an intimate, vital and indispensable role.

Given the prevalence of these canonistic assumptions, it was easy enough for publicist writers like the Dominican, John of Paris, in the early fourteenth century, or Pierre d'Ailly and Nicholas of Cusa, during the councils of Constance and Basel, to build upon them and to look to the Sacred College for the imposition of some continuously operating constitutional restraint upon the pope. Thus John of Paris, in his *Tractatus de potestate regia et papali,* argued that the cardinals, who acted on behalf of the universal Church in electing the pope, could equally well act on its behalf in deposing him.[23] Earlier in the same tract he had

21. Brian Tierney, *Foundations of the Conciliar Theory* (Cambridge, 1958), p. 184.
22. *Ibid.,* p. 117.
23. *Tractatus,* ch. 24; in J. Leclercq, *Jean de Paris et l'ecclésiologie du XIIIe siècle* (Paris, 1924), p. 254; cf. the other texts cited in Tierney, *Foundations,* p. 176, n. 2.

argued that the best and most practicable form of government for the Church would be that form of kingship which contains an admixture of aristocracy and democracy as well—such a regimen being best because all elements of the community have some part in it.[24] But if John did not go on to identify with the cardinals the aristocratic element in his ideal ecclesiastical constitution, Pierre d'Ailly did. "It seems manifest," he tells us, using John's words, "that it would be the best regimen for the Church if, under one pope, many men were elected by and from every province," and (going one step beyond John) that "such men should be cardinals, who, with the pope and under him, might rule the Church and temper the use of the *plenitudo potestatis*."[25] And while Nicholas of Cusa does not seem to have been impressed with d'Ailly's vision of the Church as a "mixed monarchy" he did borrow from him the notion that the cardinals should serve as representatives of the church provinces, assisting the pope in the day to day government of the universal Church, whence, he adds, echoing an old canonistic phrase, they are commonly said to be "part of the pope's body".[26]

Thus far, not too precise. Elsewhere, it is true, d'Ailly goes into greater detail in his attempt to pinpoint the role of the cardinals as successors in Church government to the "Sacred College or Senate of the Apostles". In so doing, he draws heavily on the oligarchic tradition in canonistic thinking, but in this he is not as systematic as Zabarella who gives that tradition a forceful and classic expression. Though the pope is said to possess the plenitude of power, Zabarella argues, that does not mean that he alone can do everything. The expression "apostolic see" does not refer to the pope alone, but to the pope and cardinals who to-

24. *Tractatus*, ch. 19, ed. Leclercq, pp. 236-237.
25. *Tract. de eccl. pot.;* Dupin, II, col. 946; cf. Oakley, *Political Thought of Pierre d'Ailly*, pp. 118-119.
26. *De concordantia catholica*, II, 18; ed., Gerhardus Kollen (Hamburg, 1963), p. 199; cf. the analysis of Paul Sigmund, *Nicholas of Cusa and Medieval Political Thought* (Cambridge, Massachusetts, 1963), pp. 167-168, where the parallel texts are cited.

gether form a single body of which the pope is the head and the cardinals the members. Hence, if, under the present deplorable circumstances of schism, the pope refuses to summon a general council, then that right devolves upon the cardinals. Similarly, under any circumstances, "without the cardinals the pope cannot establish a general law concerning the whole Church." [27] Nor without consulting the cardinals can he take action in matters of importance. On the other hand, if circumstances warrant it, the cardinals can exert their authority to the extent of withdrawing allegiance from the pope. And during a vacancy or even a "quasi-vacancy" (which occurs when a pope cannot effectively rule the Church), they succeed to the full power of the Apostolic See. For, after all, they represent the universal Church and can act in its place.[28]

This last assertion is an important one. It expresses a sentiment that was not uncommon at the time and it helps to explain how men like John of Paris, d'Ailly and Zabarella, though they stressed the supreme authority in the Church of the general council, could align themselves also with the oligarchic curialist position that was in others so often opposed to the Conciliar theory. For it points to the fact that if Zabarella (and, less clearly, d'Ailly) saw the (local) Roman church or Apostolic See as itself a corporate body composed of pope and cardinals— with all that that implied constitutionally—they also saw it as the head, in turn, of a greater corporate body, the universal Church, from which it derived its authority and the well-being of which it existed to promote.[29]

With this we come to the third strand in Conciliarist thinking, a strand which, if it was perhaps less dominant than the almost universal belief that reform could be achieved only by resort to

27. *Acutissimi Jurisconsulti Francisci Zabarellis Cardinalis Florentini* . . . *de ejus temporis Schismate Tractatus* (Argentorati, 1609), p. 558.

28. Here, I paraphrase Tierney, *Foundations*, p. 234; cf. the whole analysis of Zabarella's position (pp. 220-237).

29. For a concise appraisal, see Tierney, *Foundations*, pp. 236-237.

the *via concilii,* was certainly more prominent at Constance and Basel than the curialist oligarchic position. This third strand, to avoid confusion, we will continue to refer to as "the strict Conciliar theory".

This strict Conciliar theory has often been misunderstood. It possessed no monolithic unity. Even if one avoids the fatal trap of confusing it with the type of Conciliarism espoused earlier on by Marsilius of Padua, one will find that the version dominant at Constance and Basel itself took more than one form. But common to all of them was the belief that the pope, however divinely-instituted his office, was not an absolute monarch but in some sense a constitutional ruler; that he possessed a merely ministerial authority delegated to him by the community of the faithful for the good of the whole Church; that that community had not exhausted its inherent authority in the mere act of electing its ruler but had retained whatever residual power was necessary to prevent its own subversion or destruction; that it could exercise that power via its representatives assembled in a general council, could do so in certain critical cases even against the wishes of the pope, and, in such cases, could proceed if need be to judge, chastise and even depose the pope.

Around this shared pattern of belief the various Conciliar thinkers wove theories of differing dimensions and textures. The differences involved reflect the differing temperaments of their authors. They reflect also the differing vocations—theologian, curial official, canonist—which had helped shape them. They reflect, again, the differing circumstances under which these men wrote—the confused year or two immediately consequent upon the onset of schism, the vigorous decade of Pisa and Constance when energies were focussed and hope ran high, or the tense years from 1431–34, when the Council of Basel was bringing Eugenius IV to heel and when Nicholas of Cusa was finishing the greatest of all the Conciliar tracts, the *De Concordantia Catholica.*

These differences can only be illustrated here. Thus when

68

Zabarella confronts the big legal obstacle facing all the Conciliarists—namely, the canonistic provision that the pope alone
can summon a general council—he chooses to do so not by
appealing, as do many of the other Conciliar theorists, to the
meta-juristic notion of equity (*epieikeia*), that is, to the spirit of
the law rather than to the letter. Instead, as befits an expert canonist, he invokes the standard canonistic teaching on the assembly
of other corporate bodies in the Church and extends it to cover
this particular case.[30] Or again, on the definition of a general
council. Whereas Conrad of Gelnhausen, on this matter strongly
influenced by Ockham, can define a general council as an assembly composed of representatives of all the different estates, ranks,
sexes and persons of Christendom, Nicholas of Cusa—in this,
despite his doctrine of universal consent, much more conservative
—sees it as essentially a general asembly of bishops which includes the Bishop of Rome.[31] Yet again, on the matter of voting
rights at the council, while Gerson is most insistent that the right
to vote be enjoyed by the lower clergy as well as by the bishops,
he is willing to see the laity restricted to a merely consultative or
advisory capacity. D'Ailly, on the other hand, argues that though
the unlearned and those of the lowest ranks are not specifically
summoned to the council, no Catholic should be excluded. Nor
should kings, princes or their ambassadors be denied a vote, any
more than should doctors of theology or of canon or civil law,
since these are all men with authority over the people.[32]

And so on. The differences undoubtedly exist, but they range

30. See the analyses of Tierney, *Foundations,* pp. 224-225, and of Ullmann,
Origins, p. 199.

31. Thus Conrad, *Epistola concordiae,* in E. Martène and V. Durand,
Thesaurus Novus Anecdotorum (Paris, 1717), II, cols. 1217-1218; Nichols of
Cusa, *De concordantia catholica,* II, 1, and III, 14; ed., Kollen, pp. 93-94
and 385. Cf. the analysis of Sigmund, *Nicholas of Cusa,* p. 161.

32. Gerson, *De pot. eccl.,* Dupin, II, 250C; cf. his *Sermo: 'Ambulate
dum lucem habetis', ibid.,* 205C. D'Ailly, *Oratio de officio imperatoris,*
Dupin, II, 921; *Disputatio de jure suffragii quibus competat,* in H. von der
Hardt, *Rerum concilii oecumenici Constantiencis* (Leipzig, 1697 ff.), II,
pp. 225-227.

only within certain fairly clearly defined limits. In particular, it should be noted that they do not extend to a denial of the divine foundation of the papal office.[33] Even Dietrich of Niem, whose anti-papalism is so extreme, and whose thinking betrays more signs of Marsilian influence than does that of any other Conciliar theorist, does not deny that. How could he? If he was concerned to reform and purify the current papal administration which he attacked so very bitterly, he was also concerned to see unity restored to the Church under one undoubted Vicar of Christ.[34] And if he argues that the general council "can take away the papal rights" since the pope is bound to obey it "in all things",[35] or if he is Marsilian enough to regard as questionable the type of "coercive power" claimed by the popes of his day, most of his fellow Conciliar theorists active at the time of Pisa and Constance were somewhat less radical—as, indeed, was Nicholas of Cusa later on.[36] Indeed, Gerson, d'Ailly, Zabarella, the other leading exponents of the strict Conciliar theory at the Council of Constance, would all of them have to be classified as moderates. And it is important to grasp this fact; upon the accuracy of our understanding of their position depends the rectitude of our interpretation of the Constance decrees *Haec sancta* and *Frequens*. At the risk, therefore, of some repetition, the position of these three men must be subjected to a somewhat closer analysis.[37]

33. Although Jean Courtecuisse, following the more sceptical strand in Ockham's thinking, is dubious about the scriptural warranty of the pope's coercive jurisdictional power. See De Lagarde, *Naissance*, V, pp. 329-330.

34. *De modis uniendi ac reformandi ecclesiae*, ed. Heimpel.

35. *Ibid.*

36. See the analysis of Sigmund, *Nicholas of Cusa*, esp. ch. 4, pp. 158-187.

37. This analysis is based upon an examination of the following works: Zabarella, *Tractatus de schismate* (see above, p. 67, n. 27), all of Pierre d'Ailly's Conciliar tracts but especially *Tractatus de ecclesiastica potestate*, *Tractatus de materia concilii generalis, and Propositiones utiles*, and Gerson's *De potestate ecclesiastica, De auferabilitate papae, Tractatus de unitate ecclesiae, Sermo 'Prosperum iter faciet nobis deus'* and *Sermo 'Ambulate dum lucem habetis'*. Of the numerous secondary works on these men the following may be referred to: Tierney, *Foundations*, pp. 220-237, and Ullmann, *Origins*, pp. 191-231 (both of these being essays on Zabarella), Oakley,

Their basic assumption, of course, is the divine institution of all ecclesiastical power. This power they divide, in accordance with the tradition, into power of orders and power of jurisdiction. About the former they have very little to say. It may well come from above. It may well leave on the souls of those who possess it an indelible character that the authority even of a general council is powerless to efface. But, then, the pope does not base his pre-eminence in the Church on his possession of orders. How could he, indeed? The papacy is not a distinct sacerdotal order; nor does the pope possess the power of orders in any degree higher than the other bishops. His claims to invulnerability rest, and have to rest, upon the nature of his jurisdictional power,[38] and, more precisely, on his power of jurisdiction in the external forum— the coercive, truly governmental power which pertains not to any merely voluntary society, but to the public authority, and which, it will be recalled, was taken also to include the magisterial power. And it is this type of jurisdictional power, and this alone, that these Conciliar theorists have in mind when they assert the superiority of council to pope. For not even the highest of papalists would deny that the pope was subject to ecclesiastical jurisdiction in the internal forum (did he, too, not have his confessor?); and not even the most radical of Conciliarists would claim that the general council *as such* was endowed with the power of orders.

It is upon an analysis of this jurisdictional power and of the precise manner in which it was distributed throughout the ranks of the faithful that these men bend, therefore, their efforts. Against the claims of the high papalists they deny that the full-

Political Thought of Pierre d'Ailly, and John B. Morrall, *Gerson and the Great Schism* (Manchester, 1960). Zabarella, writing a canonistic treatise with a very specific objective does not range as widely as do the others. What is explicit in them is sometimes only implicit in him. But I do not think I misrepresent his views here.

38. Though he would agree with this statement, Gerson does insist that the *plenitudo potestatis* cannot simply be grounded in jurisdictional power alone; see *De pot. eccl.,* Dupin, II, 239C-D.

71

ness of that power (*plenitudo potestatis*) resides in the pope alone. They do not wish thereby to deny the divine origin of the papal primacy; nor, indeed do they wish the council to encroach any more than absolutely necessary upon the normal day-to-day working of the papal monarchy. Nevertheless, though the office itself is of divine institution, its bestowal upon a particular individual is the work of men. And when the cardinals elect a pope they do so, not in their own right, but as representatives of the community of the faithful. For the final authority in the Church, as in other more particular corporations, resides in the whole body of its members.

Nor is that authority exhausted by the mere act of electing a head. Even after a papal election—and all agree on this—the fullness of power still resides in some sense in the Church as well as in the pope. So that, as Zabarella puts it, the plenitude of power is fundamentally in the whole Church as in a corporate body, and derivatively in the pope as in the "principal minister" of that corporation.[39] Or, in d'Ailly's more obscure formulation, even if the plenitude of power belongs "properly speaking" to the pope alone, since he is the one who generally exercises it, and, as a result, is possessed by the Church or the general council representing it only "figuratively and in some equivocal way", it must nevertheless be said to belong *inseparably* to the body of the Church and *representatively* to the general council, but only *separably* to the pope who is the *subject* who receives it and the *minister* who exercises it.[40] Or again, in Gerson's terms, the plenitude of power is in the whole Church and the council representing it as in the goal to which it is ordained, as in the medium through which power is conferred on individual office-holders, as in the means by which the use of that power is regulated. Thus, although the fullness of power may be ascribed to the pope in that he is superior to any other single ecclesiastic, he is not

39. *Tractatus de schismate*, 559-560.
40. *Tract. de eccl. pot.*, Dupin, II, 945-946, 950-951.

superior to the whole Church or to the general council representing it. Hence it follows that the council can set limits to his exercise of that power in order to prevent his abusing it to the
destruction of the Church.[41]

Not very clear statements, it is true, but given the frequent
references to the normal procedures followed in the ecclesiastical
corporations of the day, clearer, no doubt, to contemporaries
than to us. As *affiliated* arguments reveal, these statements are
designed above all to support the basic Conciliar contentions
that while the fullness of power is normally exercised by the pope,
it is to be used for no other end but the good of the whole Church,
and that the Church or the general council representing it re-
tains, therefore, the right to prevent its abuse.

This right is conceived as being exercised both under emergency conditions and on a more continuing basis. The emergency
situation most readily envisaged (though by no means the only
one) is that which occurs when a pope lapses into heresy, or, by
being the occasion of schism, endangers the faith of the whole
Church. Under such conditions the whole Church, which unlike
the pope possesses the gift of doctrinal inerrancy, possesses also
the power to prevent its own ruin. Hence, even though infallibility is not necessarily to be ascribed to the doctrinal decision of a
general council, in the determination of orthodoxy it certainly
does possess an authority superior to that of the pope and can,
therefore, stand in judgment over him, correct him and even, if
necessary, go so far as to depose him.

When it comes to the exercise of this inherent ecclesiastical
authority under non-emergency conditions, these Conciliar theorists are not as precise. All regarded the College of Cardinals as
sharing with the pope in the exercise of the reduced plenitude of
power which they allotted to him and as functioning, therefore,
as a continuously operating institutional restraint on the abuse

41. Just as can any other corporation in relation to its head. See Gerson,
De pot. eccl., Dupin, II, 243.

73

of that power. But, beyond that, they also envisaged some sort of continuing role for the general council. This is certainly true in matters which concern the faith and also, it would seem, in decisions which affect the general state or well-being of the Church. "What touches all must be approved by all"—or, as d'Ailly reformulated that legal maxim—"at least by many and by the more notable ones." [42] At least for him and for Gerson, general councils regularly assembled were to become a permanent rather than an exceptional part of the structure of Church government. As early as 1403, d'Ailly had anticipated *Frequens* by urging that councils in the future should assemble automatically every thirty or forty years with or without special mandate from the pope.[43]

(c) *The Constance Decrees* Haec sancta *and* Frequens

There are good reasons for believing that the position we have just summarized represents the "centrist" position at Constance and the position most widely held among the council fathers in 1415 when the decree *Haec sancta* was unanimously approved. It was certainly echoed by a variety of fathers, ranging from the distinguished cardinal, Fillastre, to Frederick of Parsberg, canon of Ratisbon. If it did not quite go far enough for the most radical of Conciliarists present at the council, it clearly went too far for the more conservative—notably some of the cardinals, who, though they had refused in March 1415 to join John XXII in abandoning the council, still had some misgivings about the course events were taking. But, as the various interventions reveal, the reason was in both cases the same—the traditional pre-

42. *Additio circa tertium viam supratactam,* In Franz Ehrle, *Martin de Alpartils Chronica Actitatorum,* I, Quellen und Forschungen aus dem Gebiete der Geschichte, VII (Paderborn, 1906), p. 506. The maxim itself is drawn from the Roman law.

43. *Tractatus de materia,* ed. Oakley, *Political Thought of Pierre d'Ailly,* p. 317. For the similar suggestion of Gerson's, see John B. Morrall, *Gerson and the Great Schism* (Manchester, 1960), p. 98.

rogatives of the cardinals—and it had nothing to do, strictly speaking, with the affirmation of the strict Conciliar theory. For the more radical thinkers, the College of Cardinals was too thoroughly discredited and itself too badly in need of reform to be accorded here and now a constitutional role in the limitation of papal power analogous to that claimed for the council. For some of the cardinals, on the other hand, imbued as they were with the oligarchic curialist tradition, circumstances at the time were not yet of sufficient gravity to make it necessary to appeal beyond the Roman church (and, indeed, against it) to that residual authority in the universal Church which, as they themselves were willing to admit, a general council could in certain cases exercise.[44]

The position shared by Gerson, d'Ailly and Zabarella clearly occupied middle ground between these opposing attitudes, and Paul de Vooght has contended that it is this moderate stance that is reflected in the provisions of the decree *Haec sancta.* The text of the decree bears out, I believe, his contention. The main section reads as follows:

This sacred synod of Constance . . . declares, in the first place, that it forms a general council representing the Catholic Church, that it has its power immediately from Christ, and that all men, of every rank and position, including the pope himself, are bound to obey it in those matters that pertain to the faith, the extirpation of the said schism, and to the reformation of the said Church in head and members. It declares also that anyone, of any rank, condition or office—even the papal—who shall contumaciously refuse to obey the mandates, statutes, decrees or instructions made by this holy synod or by any other lawfully assembled council on the matters aforesaid or on things pertaining to them, shall, unless he recovers his senses, be subjected to fitting penance and punished as is appropriate. . . .[45]

44. For an analysis of the relevant memoranda and interventions, see Paul de Vooght, *Les pouvoirs du Concile et l'autorité du pape au Concile de Constance* (Paris, 1965), pp. 40-54.
45. J. Mansi, *Sacrorum conciliorum nova et amplissima collectio* (Florence, 1759 ff.), XXVII, pp. 590 ff.

75

What is involved here is clearly a statement of the strict Conciliar theory. The decree affirms the contention basic to that theory that, under certain circumstances, the general council, acting alone, is possessed of an authority superior to that of any of the faithful, including the pope himself. Furthermore, the second clause makes it clear that the superiority claimed for the council is a superiority claimed not just for Constance but for all legitimately assembled general councils. It makes it clear, too, that the circumstances it has in mind are not merely the grievous circumstances of the moment but comparable circumstances in the future. And its definition of those circumstances is remarkably wide, for it involves the affirmation of Conciliar supremacy, not only under temporary conditions of emergency, but also on a more enduring basis. That definition, indeed, is somewhat wider than Zabarella seems to have wished. It involves the ascription to the council of a superior jurisdiction not merely in matters of faith and schism (with which he heartily agreed), but also in matters relating to the reform of the Church in head and members and even "in matters pertaining" thereto. With this last assertion Zabarella was certainly unhappy. In the fourth general session of the council, held on March 30, 1415, he had read to the fathers, and supported, a version of the first article of *Haec sancta* which coincided with the final version adopted except for the fact that the reference to "reformation in head and members" was omitted. And, according to Cardinal Fillastre, though Zabarella was present at the fifth session when *Haec sancta* was adopted, he refused to read the text to the council—presumably because he still doubted either the legality or the wisdom of reinstating the clause which asserted the further subordination of pope to council in all matters pertaining to reform of the Church in head and members.[46]

46. See Fillastre's *Diary of the Council of Constance,* trans. L. R. Loomis, in J. H. Mundy and K. M. Woody, *The Council of Constance* (New York, 1961), pp. 227-229. See also the account of the crucial third, fourth and fifth sessions in C. J. Hefele, *Histoire des Conciles d'après les documents*

Apart from this, however, *Haec sancta* clearly claimed nothing more for the council than moderates like Zabarella, d'Ailly and Gerson had long since claimed. It was neither "the hasty product of a day" nor a revolutionary manifesto that simply reflected the views of Conciliarist radicals. But what, then, of *Frequens,* the second great decree which the council promulgated two years later in 1417? It imposed upon the pope, as a matter of legal obligation, the assembly in the future of general councils at stated and regular intervals. But perhaps because this decree was promulgated by the whole council in the presence even of those cardinals (including the future Martin V) who had fled with the ill-fated John XXIII, or perhaps because it can be related as easily to what we have called the first strand in Conciliarist thinking as to the strict Conciliar theory, there has not been that much argument about its validity. And yet, if we remember that *Haec sancta* decreed the subordination of pope to council not merely in the particular emergency of the day or in comparable future emergencies, but also on a more enduring basis, it would seem that *Frequens* should be read as an attempt to translate into a disciplinary regulation the conviction underlying *Haec sancta.* The question of its validity, therefore, is bound up with the greater question of the dogmatic validity of that decree. The fact that *Haec sancta* was the expression of views long held by the moderates among the Conciliar theorists is, of course, relevant to this matter of validity. But so, too, are the source and subsequent fate of those views. Before broaching the much-disputed question of validity, then, and abandoning thereby the historical perspective for the ecclesiological, it will be necessary to address ourselves to these prior but related matters.

---

originaux, trans. and ed. H. Leclercq (Paris, 1907 ff.), VII, pp. 197-213, but note the necessary correction of Hefele's account of Zabarella's activity in de Vooght, *Les pouvoirs du Concile,* p. 32, n. 7.

CHAPTER 3

The Career of Conciliarism

(a) The Importance of Origins

Simply to claim a Marsilian origin for the Conciliarism of Constance is no longer possible. However reassuring it may be for those who have felt obliged to discredit the Conciliar theorists as having attempted to foist on the Church an unorthodox ecclesiology of revolutionary vintage, that claim has been unable to stand up under historical examination. That it should have gained any credence at all must be attributed primarily to the complexity of Conciliarism and its concomitant susceptibility to misrepresentation. There were at least three strands to the Conciliarist thinking of the classical era, and, as we have seen,[1] two of those strands had unimpeachably orthodox origins amid the cozy respectabilities of the pre-Marsilian era. But what of the third —the strict Conciliar theory—the strand that concerns us most directly? To what extent can it lay claim to origins more weighty than the disruptive incoherences of the period of schism but at the same time more respectable than the blunt negations of a Marsilius or the convoluted anti-papalisms of an Ockham?

Until a few years ago it would have been hard, indeed, to answer that question. When discussing the oligarchic curialist tradition, we noted that the theoretical roots of that tradition plunged deep into the commentaries on the canon law produced by generations of church lawyers.[2] Over the years, scholars working on the Conciliarist literature of the classical era—or, indeed, on

---

1. See above, ch. 2, pp. 61 ff.
2. See above, ch. 2, pp. 64-65.

forerunners like Ockham or John of Paris—more than once had occasion to note the frequency with which canonistic citations appeared even in tracts that showed no sympathy with that oligarchic tradition. But it is only in the last few decades, with the growth of interest in the history of medieval canon law, that the importance of those citations has become clear and the profound indebtedness of the Conciliar theorists to the teaching of the canon lawyers has been realized. And though he was able to build on the suggestions and arguments of a series of earlier scholars, credit for the decisive contribution still must go to Brian Tierney, whose book, *Foundations of the Conciliar Theory*, published in 1955, marked something of a turning point in Conciliar studies.[3]

The case Tierney makes is a strong one. It is grounded firmly in an intensive examination of canonistic materials, much of them unprinted, and the tide of literature on Conciliar matters that has been flowing in the last few years has done nothing to shake it. At its heart lies the assertion that the strict Conciliar theory, far from being a reaction against canonistic views or a profane importation onto ecclesial soil, was in fact the logical outgrowth of certain strands of canonist thought itself. In the first place, it was the outcome of the attempts of generations of canonists from the late-thirteenth century onwards to rationalize the structure both of the individual churches of Christendom and of the universal Church itself. During the centuries preceding the schism two separate doctrines of Church unity had been developed by the canonists.

---

3. *Foundations of the Conciliar Theory: The Contribution of the Medieval Canonists from Gratian to the Great Schism* (Cambridge, 1955). Tierney is Professor of Medieval History at Cornell University and a past president of the American Catholic Historical Association. In connection with this book should also be consulted Tierney's subsequent article, "Pope and Council: Some New Decretist Texts," *Mediaeval Studies*, XIX (1957), 197-218. The observations which follow are based largely upon these works and upon James M. Moynihan, *Papal Immunity and Liability in the Writings of the Medieval Canonists* (Rome, 1961).

The more conspicuous one, which has usually been regarded as the canonistic doctrine *par excellence* insisted that the unity of the whole Church could be secured only by a rigorous subordination of all the members to a single head, and to make that subordination effective, it developed the familiar theory of papal sovereignty. But side by side with this there existed another theory, applied at first to the single churches and then, at the beginning of the fourteenth century, in a fragmentary fashion, to the Roman church and the Church as a whole, a theory which stressed the corporate association of the members of a Church as the true principle of ecclesiastical unity, and which envisaged an exercise of corporate authority by the members of the church even in the absence of an effective head.[4]

And if the members of the Church through the agency of the cardinals had endowed the pope with authority, it remained their prerogative, should he fall into error on a matter of faith or abuse his authority in a manner detrimental to the common good of the whole Church, to withdraw that authority.

It is this latter theory, of course, that is expressed so forcefully in Gerson and d'Ailly, and, with such a wealth of canonistic citation, in Zabarella. Their arguments, however, draw also upon another and older strand in canonistic thinking, one that goes back to the commentaries written upon the *Decretum* of Gratian in the twelfth and early-thirteenth centuries, and, above all, to their discussions of the case of the heretical pope. The "Decretists", or commentators on the *Decretum,* denied to the pope himself, and to the (local) Roman church of pope and cardinals, the prerogative of inerrancy which they accorded to the universal Church. On the basis of this, some of them (most notably the author of the *glossa ordinaria*—the influential standard commentary on the *Decretum*) concluded that the general council must be "above the pope" in matters of faith. By this they probably meant no more than that on those matters the decisions of pope and council acting together, as they normally would, were superior to the decisions of the pope alone. But what if a pope

4. Tierney, *Foundations,* p. 240.

lapsed into heresy? Gratian had included in the *Decretum* the ancient legal maxim, which, although it is now known to stem from a sixth-century forgery, still remains enshrined in the 1917 *Code of Canon Law*—namely, that "the pope can be judged by no one".[5] He had also included, however, the qualification appended to that maxim during the eleventh century—namely, "unless he [the pope] is caught deviating from the faith". But if the pope is indeed accused of heresy (or, for that matter, of any notorious crime tantamount to heresy), by whom will he be judged? There was no one single Decretist theory on this point and many important canonistic texts still await assessment. There seem, however, to have been two main schools of thought. According to the one, a pope who lapsed into heresy ceased *ipso facto* to be pope. If he contumaciously persisted in his heresy recourse to a judicial superior might be necessary in order to make it clear that he was, in fact, guilty of heresy and in order to have proclaimed, therefore, a *declaratory* sentence of deposition. But that judicial superior might be the College of Cardinals and not the general council. The principal spokesman of this school of thought was Huguccio (d. 1210). According to the other school, an heretical pope did not cease *ipso facto* to be pope; he had instead to be subjected to trial, judgment and deposition. And the body possessing the requisite superior authority enabling it to stand in judgment was the general council since, even acting in opposition to the pope, it possessed a superior jurisdiction in matters pertaining to the faith. The chief advocate of this point of view was Alanus. On this crucial point, the teaching of Johannes Teutonicus (d. 1246), author of the influential *glossa ordinaria,* is ambiguous. But it was understood by many to back the latter school of thought, and, certainly, even in "the most cautious glosses" of the late-thirteenth and fourteenth centuries that latter school prevailed. In those glosses

5. *Decretum Gratiani,* D. 40, ch. 6; ed. A. Friedberg, *Corpus Juris Canonici* (Leipzig, 1879-81), I, p. 146. *Codex Juris Canonici* (1917), can. 1556.

there was little trace of Huguccio's cautious distinctions indicating that a pope had ceased to be pope before being brought to trial, and thus eliminating the necessity of a strict papal trial as such. Rather, the conciliarist doctrine of Alanus came to the fore during this period, and his view was [later] presented in a cogent synthesis by the great canonist, Franciscus Zabarella.[6]

It is in the combination of *both* of these strands of canonistic thinking—the second "corporatist" view of Church unity and the latter "Decretist" theory of papal liability—that we find the foundation of the strict Conciliar theory. And it is necessary to insist on this fact because August Franzen, who has recently argued, in an essay that is likely to be widely read, that Tierney's thesis has been misunderstood by those seeking to vindicate the dogmatic validity of *Haec sancta,* simply ignores the whole corporatist strand with its stress on the continuing authority of the body of the faithful, and confines himself, instead, to discussing the Decretist teaching on the case of the heretical pope.[7] And this teaching he misrepresents somewhat by implying that the canonists refrained from according to the general council a genuine jurisdictional authority over the pope even in matters of faith, on the grounds that an heretical pope would have ceased *ipso facto* to be pope and that the council in judging him was merely involved in proclaiming a declaratory sentence on a private individual who was no longer anything more than a "pseudo-pope". As we have seen, this was the point of view defended by only one of the Decretist schools of thought on the subject, and that school not the one which prevailed in the century preceding the outbreak of schism.

In discussing the strict Conciliar theory, then, it would be difficult to overestimate the importance of this matter of origins. We have argued that the decrees of Constance reflect the moderate version of Conciliar theory expressed so notably in the works

6. Moynihan, *Papal Immunity,* p. 142.
7. August Franzen, "The Council of Constance: Present State of the Problem," *Concilium* (Glen Rock, New Jersey, 1965), VII, pp. 46 ff., 63 ff.

82

of Gerson d'Ailly and Zabarella. It may now be added that the strict Conciliar theory itself faithfully enshrined in turn the teaching of generations of canonists. That theory and those decrees must be regarded, therefore, not as "something accidental or external, thrust upon the Church from outside" but rather "as a logical culmination of ideas that were imbedded in the law and doctrine of the Church itself".[8] And their dogmatic status must be assessed accordingly.

(b) The Papalist Reaction: Eugenius IV to Leo X

If it has been the achievement of recent historical studies to have made it abundantly clear that the Conciliar theory which dominated Pisa, Constance and Basel was not as recent or revolutionary in its origins as it once was usual to assume, it is tempting to jump to the congruent conclusion that the demise of that theory was probably neither as sudden nor as final as formerly we were led to suppose. And yet, the last years of the Conciliar movement are hardly very reassuring on this score. These are the years, after all, that witnessed the defection to Eugenius of some of the most prominent supporters of the Council of Basel—notably Cesarini, its former president, and Nicholas of Cusa, the most famous of all Conciliar theorists. These are the years, too, that witnessed Eugenius IV's questioning in the bulls *Moyses vir Dei* (1439) and *Etsi non dubitemus* (1441), of the legitimacy of *Haec sancta.* These are the years, again, that saw the triumphant promulgation by the Council of Florence on July 6, 1439, of *Laetentur coeli,* the decree of union with the Greeks, which concluded with the definition of the Roman primacy that was to be a model for the comparable definition promulgated by the First Vatican Council. It went as follows:

8. The words are Tierney's (*Foundations,* p. 13), but are written in relation to the Conciliar movement in general.

. . . We define that the holy Apostolic See and the Roman Pontiff hold the primacy over the whole world, that the Roman Pontiff himself is the successor of Peter, prince of the Apostles, that he is the true vicar of Christ, head of the whole Church, father and teacher of all Christians; and [we define] that to him in [the person of] Peter was given by our Lord Jesus Christ the full power of nourishing, ruling and governing the universal Church; as it is also contained in the acts of the ecumenical councils and in the holy canons.[9]

Jedin, who contends that "this definition was the answer to Basel's attempt to erect the Conciliar theory into a dogma", says also that "it became the *Magna Carta* of the papal restoration".[10] And, certainly, the progress of that restoration was very marked in the years that ensued. These years were distinguished by the progressive transformation of the papal states into a strong Italian principality, by the growth in prestige of the papal court as a center of humanist enlightenment and artistic patronage, and by the strengthening within the Church of the high-papalist interpretation of the papal monarchy. The strict Conciliar theory was by no means dead and appeals from existing papal policies to the judgment of a future general council were frequent. But by the latter part of the fifteenth century the popes felt strong enough to try to eliminate this "execrable abuse". And in January 1460 Pius II prohibited in the bull *Execrabilis* any future appeals of this type, condemning them as "erroneous end detestable".[11]

This prohibition Pius II himself renewed in November of the same year. In 1483 and 1509, respectively, Sixtus IV and Julius II followed suit. When the persistence of such appeals led finally in 1511 to the assembly at Pisa of a dissident anti-papal *concilia-*

9. Denzinger, *Enchiridion Symbolorum,* ed. A. Schönmetzer (33rd. ed.; Rome, 1965), § 1307, 332.

10. Hubert Jedin, *A History of the Council of Trent,* trans. Ernest Graf (St. Louis, 1957), I, pp. 19-20. Jedin's remarks prejudge, of course, the question of the dogmatic status of *Haec sancta.* For a discussion of his position on that question, see below, ch. 4, pp. 113 ff.

11. Denzinger, Schönmetzer, § 1375, 345.

bulum under the auspices of the French king, Julius II and, after him, Leo X were able to undercut its strength by assembling a rival council. This council, in that it was a purely episcopal body and clearly under papal domination, combined the models of the ancient and high-medieval general councils. Though some theologians in the sixteenth and seventeenth centuries expressed doubts about its status, it is nowadays customary to include this assembly, the Fifth Lateran Council, among those councils generally recognized by the Roman Catholic Church as ecumenical. And the bull *Pastor aeternus,* which that council promulgated in 1516, stated that the pope, having authority over all councils, had the right to convoke, transfer and dissolve them. So that, according to Jedin, "to the [previous] papal prohibition of appeal to a Council was now added a condemnation of the [Conciliar] theory itself".[12] The papal triumph, therefore, would seem now to have been complete.

(c) "Silver-Age" Conciliarism

Within the following year, of course, Luther was to launch his great protest. But given the closing of ranks that was to occur during the Counter-Reformation era, it would still be easy to assume that the road from *Laetentur coeli* and *Pastor aeternus* to Vatican I could only be a direct and untroubled one. This was not, in fact, to be the case, and Jedin, again, makes clear why this should be so. Thus, though he stresses the triumph of the papacy over the Conciliarists at Basel, he is also at pains to describe, and in considerable detail, the survival of Conciliar theory right on into the sixteenth century. Again, though he emphasizes the impressive progress of papal restoration in the decades after Basel, he does not overlook the presence "within the restored papacy" of debilitating tensions that were partly constitutional in nature.

12. Denzinger, Schönmetzer, § 1445, 355-356; Jedin, *History,* I, p. 133.

But if the picture which emerges is a complex and often confusing one, it may be suggested that these complexities correspond, and to a marked degree, with the complexities of Conciliarist thinking itself. Once this is realized, the confusion, if it cannot wholly be dispelled, can at least be diminished. For the three strands which were woven together in the Conciliarist thinking of the classical era, just as they had been distinct in their origins, were distinct also in their subsequent careers.

The second strand, it will be recalled,[13] envisaged the constitution of the Church in oligarchic terms, the pope being limited in his power, not by the general council, but by the cardinals. The source of this oligarchic view, it will also be recalled, lay in the traditions of the Roman *curia,* and its synthesis with the third strand, the more democratic strict Conciliar theory, came only during the years of schism and then really fully only in the works of Zabarella and d'Ailly. The synthesis was not a very stable one and the years after the collapse of Basel witnessed its disintegration.

This did not mean, however, that the old curialist oligarchic tradition itself disappeared. What it meant, instead, was that that tradition found its home again where it had found it before, not among the advocates of the strict Conciliar theory but in the Roman *curia* itself. There D'Ailly's writings exerted, it would seem, an enduring influence, and men who would have no truck with his strict Conciliar theorizing eagerly espoused his oligarchic views. The most prominent of these men was the high papalist Juan de Torquemada (d. 1468), who served to hand on d'Ailly's views to generations of curialists, since much of the discussion in his great *Summa de ecclesia* (*ca.* 1453) of the cardinalate is taken verbatim, though naturally without acknowledgment, from d'Ailly's *Tractatus de ecclesiastica potestate.* The advocacy of these views by the dean of papalists himself was itself an event of some importance, as the latter half of the fifteenth

13. See above, ch. 2, pp. 63 ff.

century saw the tensions which for a century and a half had plagued the relationship between pope and cardinals deepen into a veritable struggle for power. In this struggle, the efforts of the cardinals, perhaps because their motivation was so obviously self-centered, did not meet with much success. In an attempt to strike back against the growing absolutism of the Renaissance pope, they adopted the policy of requiring pope-elect after pope-elect to swear to the faithful observance of the rules laid down in election capitulations which the cardinals themselves drew up and which were designed, in large part, to guarantee the security of their existing position and to promote a redistribution of governmental power to their advantage. These capitulations were, doubtless, "rearguard actions not offensive strokes",[13] but they do reveal the extent to which the oligarchic tradition was still alive at the start of the sixteenth century. And that fact is underlined, too, by the tendency, widespread even among those who rejected the strict Conciliar theory, to ascribe to the cardinals a right to convoke a general council in cases of emergency even against the expressed wish of the pope.

By the start of that century, too, it had long been customary for the cardinals to include among their election capitulations the demand that a new reforming council be promptly assembled. Nor was this wholly a matter of public relations. It reveals also the desire of the cardinals to make their own (and presumably to exploit in their own particular interests) the persistent demand for reform of the Church in head and members and the continuing belief that this could best be initiated and consolidated through the periodic assembly of general councils. It will be recalled that this demand—the first and most prominent strand of the Conciliarist thinking of the classical era—had had little to do with the oligarchic view, except in the thinking of a man like d'Ailly, and, until the outbreak of schism, not a great deal more to do with the third strand, the strict Conciliar theory. Its alliance

14. Jedin, *History,* I, p. 90.

with that third strand was the product of the extraordinary circumstances of the schism, and, by the mid-fifteenth century, as
the career of Nicholas of Cusa so well illustrates, that alliance
was crumbling. In the years after Basel, those who believed that
the necessary reform in head and members could be achieved
only by means of a general council increasingly recoiled from
advocacy of the strict Conciliar theory. Their "great concern",
Jedin has pointed out, "was not so much the supremacy of the
Council as the holding of a Council there and then." [14] Hence,
when in 1511 Louis XII of France, with the help of several dissident cardinals, succeeded in securing without papal cooperation
the assembly of a council at Pisa, thereby transforming a persistently theoretical anti-papal threat into an all too practical
reality, the majority of those churchmen most interested in reform dashed his hopes by choosing to align themselves with the
Fifth Lateran Council which Julius II had convoked by way of
retaliation.

It should not be assumed, however, that adhesion to the
Lateran Council necessarily meant any rejection of the validity
of the Constance decrees. Of course, because of the use which the
initiators of the Council of Pisa made of *Frequens,* it is not
surprising that Julius II should seek, when he in turn convoked
the Lateran Council, to prevent any misunderstanding of his action by pointing out that that decree had long since lapsed into
desuetude, and that even if it had not, extenuating circumstances
would have rendered it inapplicable in his own day. Given the
context of events, what *is* surprising is the demand that general
councils be held every ten or fifteen years which the Spaniards
made at the Council (and not without reference to *Frequens*),
or, again, the similar demand made by the two Camaldolese
monks, Giustiniani and Quirini, who, in the great program for
reform which they presented to Leo X, stated quite explicitly

15. *Ibid.,* p. 61.

that they regarded it as nothing less than vital to the recovery and maintenance of the health of the Church that general councils be held every five years.

Similarly with respect to *Haec sancta.* If some of the fathers assembled at the Lateran council felt unable to accord any validity to the provisions of that decree, none of them seems to have been willing to say as much. When those who had supported Pisa sought to make their peace with the pope and to take their seats in the council, while they were required, of course, to abjure the schismatic Pisan assembly and to declare their adherence to the pope and the Lateran council, no mention was made of *Haec sancta* and no explicit rejection of Conciliar theory was required of them. Again, though the whole sermon delivered to the council by Thomas de Vio, the Dominican master general and future Cardinal Cajetan, was concerned with matters ecclesiological and conciliar, he, too, was silent on *Haec sancta.*

Elsewhere, it is true, in his De *comparatione auctoritati papae et concilii* (1511), he had been more explicit, not only insisting on the superiority of pope to council but also casting doubt on the ecumenicity of the Council of Constance in its early sessions when *Haec sancta* was promulgated. And yet, even here, his case is not as monolithic as one might expect, for, while seeking to limit its applications, he does retain some elements of the strict Conciliar position. Thus, he is willing to admit that under certain exceptional circumstances a general council can assemble itself, even against the wishes of the pope, and take whatever action is necessary to prevent the destruction of the Church. The circumstances he had in mind are those that arise when there have been one or more doubtful elections to the papacy or when a pope, the legitimacy of whose title is contested, falls into notorious and obstinate heresy. He includes among the actions necessary to meet such crises the deposition of an heretical pope, and it should be noted that what he is ascribing to the council here is an actual deposing power—a power of jurisdiction—and not merely the right to declare that a pope is in fact a heretic and has thereby ceased *ipso facto* to be pope.[16]

On this critical issue, then, there are serious hesitations even in the thinking of the man who was perhaps the most distinguished theologian of his time and certainly the most formidable adversary of the Conciliar theorists who defended Pisa. In this he was by no means unique. Similar hesitations had characterized the ecclesiology of more than one of these churchmen in the era of papal restoration whom we tend to classify as high papalists and who, unlike some modern commentators, do not seem to have thought that the general definition of the Roman primacy contained in the Florentine decree of union with the Greeks settled anything at all.[17] This is true of Torquemada himself, who certainly admitted that the council was in some cases superior to the pope. His position on these matters, though it may be in tension with his general ecclesiology, was not far removed, in fact, from Decretist attempts to cope with the case of the heretical pope.

Few would be disposed to question the enduring influence on the papalist camp of Torquemada's ideas. The reformer Quirini's *Tractatus super concilium generale,* with its provision for the deposition of heretical popes by general councils, itself indicates that that influence was very much at work among the ecclesiastics

16. He explicitly rejects this last view, even though he involves himself thereby in an intricate and implausible attempt to avoid admitting that the pope's authority is in some way inferior to that of the council; see Thomas de Vio Cardinalis Cajetanus, *De comparatione auctoritatis papae et concilii,* chs. 20-22; ed. V. M. Pollet (Rome, 1936), pp. 125 ff. Cf. the analysis in Francis Oakley, "Almain and Major: Conciliar Theory on the Eve of the Reformation," *American Historical Review,* LXX (1965), 675 ff.

17. Among these modern commentators, Joseph Gill is prominent. See his *Personalities of the Council of Florence* (New York, 1964), ch. 20, esp. pp. 264-265. For an analysis of Gill's position on the validity of the Constance decrees, see below, ch. 4, pp. 111 ff. A close reading of the relevant parts of *Laetentur coeli* reveals little in the rather general claims it makes for the papacy that a Zabarella or a d'Ailly would have balked at. Unlike the primacy definition of Vatican I it did not claim for the pope the possession of the supreme judicial power in the Church.

involved in the Lateran Council. Quirini insisted, of course, that "the pontifical authority is above the council", for this had long been the motto of those who adhered to the papalist position, but then, as de Vooght has said, their papalism was often more qualified than the slogan under which they served.[18] And this is also, it may be suggested, the background against which the formulas of *Pastor aeternus* must be judged. For about Conciliar theory that decree in fact said very little—and then only indirectly. It is concerned with the Conciliar question only at one remove. It addresses itself explicitly to no more than the papal right of convoking, transferring and dissolving councils. It does not spurn the superiority decrees of Basel, nor is there any mention of Constance or any rejection of *Haec sancta*. And this is not because such a move would have been regarded as redundant at the time, for Ferdinand the Catholic, King of Spain, in the instructions he gave to his representatives at the council had specifically suggested the need for a formal repudiation of *Haec sancta,* a repudiation which was never to occur.[19]

It is clear, then, that the adhesion of so many of the advocates of reform to the Latern Council and their lack of sympathy with the rival Conciliarist assembly at Pisa does not necessarily mean that they felt unable to accord any validity to the Conciliarist decrees of Constance. But it would still seem to indicate that they would have no truck with Conciliar theory in the form espoused by the defenders of Pisa; or, at least, that they had no sympathy with the use to which that theory was being put at Pisa. And, in fact, both suppositions are correct.

18. Paul de Vooght, "Le conciliarisme au conciles de Constance et de Bâle," in B. Botte *et al., Le Concile et les Conciles: Contribution à l'histoire de la vie conciliare de l'église* (Chevetogne-Paris, 1960), p. 175. Conciliarism at the Lateran council is the specific topic of a chapter I have contributed to a forthcoming collective volume on that council under the editorship of R. S. Schoeck (University of Toronto Press). Full references to the sources are given in that chapter.

19. Printed in José M. Doussinague, *Fernando el Católico y el cisma de Pisa* (Madrid, 1946), App. 50, p. 539.

One of the great merits of Jedin's masterly account of fifteenth-century ecclesiological developments is the degree to which it makes clear that it was the very frequency of appeals to a future general council and the very prevalence of the strict Conciliar theory that called forth prohibitions such as *Execrabilis*. Despite the defeat of the radical Conciliarists at Basel, despite the subsequent papalist reaction, despite *Execrabilis* even, the strict Conciliar theory was very much alive at the beginning of the sixteenth century. If in Spain it had fallen on characteristically stony ground, in Italy it had taken firm root, at least among the jurists, and was to find one distinguished exponent in the very court of the redoubtable Julius II himself. In France, where it enjoyed a vigorous and continuous public life, the theologians of the University of Paris claimed it as a tradition going back to the days of Constance, and forced would-be opponents to recant their views. Of the British Isles, Jedin says little—presumably because no really vital Conciliarist tradition had developed in England. Even there, however, Conciliar theory enjoyed at least a temporary vogue at the beginning of the sixteenth century, finding a clear reflection in the views of Sir Thomas More. And attention has recently been drawn to the existence in Scotland of a truly vigorous Conciliarist tradition, one which dated back to the days of Basel and which endured well into the sixteenth century.

It was from Scotland, then, as well as from France and Italy that the strict Conciliar theory was to draw its "silver-age" apologists when the assembly of Pisa transformed what had seemed like a blunted diplomatic weapon into a pointed ecclesiological threat. Notably among these apologists were the Frenchman, Jacques Almain (d. 1515), and his former teacher, the Scotsman, John Major (d. 1550). Both of these men, as representative of the Faculty of Theology at Paris, claimed that they were merely expressing the point of view traditional to their university, and, certainly, what is most strikingly revealed by a comparison of their works with the Conciliarist literature of the classical period is the element of continuity. For what we see in these tracts of Almain and Major, rigorously shaped, surrounded by many of the old arguments and buttressed by the addition of some new ones, is the strict Conciliar theory in very much the same form as it had taken in the works of d'Ailly and Gerson, their predecessors not only in the Faculty of Theology of the University of Paris but also at the Collège de Navarre within that university.[20]

They lean heavily for support upon the arguments of these predecessors and explicitly acknowledge their indebtedness to them. At first glance, certainly, this element of positive continuity is most striking. These silver-age tracts, however, are silent on certain things and one should not overlook the discontinuities which those silences reveal. There are two matters on which they are particularly revealing—nothing else, in fact, than the two other strands in the Conciliarism of the classical era: the elevated position in the Church often accorded to the cardinals, and the role assigned to the council in the reform of the Church. Thus Major has next to nothing to say about the position of the cardinals. Almain, though he notes that some predecessors like d'Ailly believed the cardinals by the institution of Christ to have succeeded to the place of the apostles in the hierarchy, himself betrays no sympathy with this belief. And both men, influenced though they are by Gerson and d'Ailly, are nevertheless quite explicit in their rejection of the idea that the Church has anything other than a strictly monarchical constitution, whether it be a democratic, aristocratic or, even, a "mixed" one.

What we are witnessing, of course, in this apparent rejection by Almain and Major of the old curialist oligarchic tradition is, once more, its separation from the strict Conciliar theory with which it had enjoyed a fleeting though by no means uneasy association. It need hardly be said that there is no similar rejection of

20. This analysis of their Conciliar arguments is based on my "Conciliar Theory on the Eve of the Reformation," 673-690.

the importance of reforming the Church in head and members, itself the most pressing problem of the day. And yet, writing on on the very eve of the Reformation, Major mentions reform but briefly, and Almain, not at all. This oversight can hardly be explained in purely personal terms. Both men spent their formative years at the Collège de Montaigu under the rigorous rule of the Flemish reformer, Jean Standonck, and there is no reason to think that they themselves were necessarily lukewarm in the matter of reform. The reason for their silence is a more fundamental one. It springs, it would seem, not from their personal predilections, but from the essentially Gallican context in which their Conciliar thinking had been framed and the essentially nationalistic purposes which it was now being used to serve.

If the strict Conciliar theory had enjoyed a vigorous and continuous public life in France, it had done so because the maintenance of this "theological Gallicanism" served that "political Gallicanism" which had become an integral part of French royal policy.[21] "The chief beneficiary" of the papal triumph over the Conciliar movement "was the modern state which during the period of conflict had got into the habit of independent action in purely ecclesiastical questions" [22]—action inspired, to a very considerable degree, by motives of a purely political hue. This habit had been formalized in France in the Pragmatic Sanction which a national assembly at Bourges issued on its own authority in June 1438 and which gave the force of law in France to some of the reform decrees of Basel. It also endorsed the Conciliarist assertion of the superiority of council to pope and it became a powerful weapon in the armoury of the French kings

---

21. Viscount St. Cyres, "The Gallican Church," *Cambridge Modern History* (New York, 1908), V, p. 75, contrasts theological Gallicanism with political Gallicanism as follows: "Theological Gallicanism maintained that the supreme infallible authority of the Church was committed to Pope and Bishops jointly. Political Gallicanism declared that no amount of misconduct, or neglect of Catholic interests, justified the Pope in interfering with a temporal sovereign."

22. Jedin, *History*, I, p. 21.

whenever they wished to apply political pressure on the papacy. The *conciliabulum* of Pisa, very much, of course, a Conciliarist council, itself serves to illustrate this fact and it should remind us that advocates of the strict Conciliar theory were no longer necessarily concerned with Church reform since, despite its formal pronouncements, the real ecclesiastical evil which that council was assembled to remedy was nothing more spiritual than the adoption by Julius II of a diplomatic stance hostile to the international ambitions of the French king.

Presumably it was this, more than anything else, that accounts for the unwillingness of reformers, who did not themselves reject the validity of the Constance decrees, to side with Almain and the Pisan assembly. And it was for analogous reasons that the continuing advocacy of Conciliarist principles by Gallican writers—and, perhaps, later on, by the advocates of "Febronianism" in Germany [23]—served only to push those principles and the memory of the Constance decrees further and further into the shadow of heterodoxy. For the strict Conciliar theory certainly lived on in the writings of the theological Gallicans. Thus, Edmond Richer, Syndic of the Sorbonne, published in 1606 a very influential edition of the works of Gerson (including also Conciliar tracts of John of Paris, d'Ailly, Major and Almain), and in 1611, his famous and controversial *Libellus de ecclesiastica et politica potestate* which relied very heavily on the Conciliar thinking of Gerson, d'Ailly, Major and Almain.

Later on in the century, Bossuet, Bishop of Meaux and architect of the Declaration of the Gallican Clergy (1682), proclaimed his adherence to the strict Conciliar theory (the Declaration, after all, had endorsed *Haec sancta*), supporting his stand by citing the views of the same four men. At the start of the next century, the example of Richer and Bossuet was followed by Louis Ellies du Pin, who not only included numerous tracts of

23. See M. O'Callaghan, *New Catholic Encyclopedia*, V, s.v. "Febronianism."

d'Ailly, Major, Almain and other Conciliarists in his 1706 edition of Gerson's complete works, but also claimed in 1707 that the University of Paris had always held "as a fundamental point of its ecclesiastical discipline" that the council is above the pope.[24]

And so on. The eighteenth century was to witness something of a decline in the fortunes of the theological Gallicans, but their writings carried the memory of the strict Conciliar theory through into the nineteenth century, when, even after 1870, it was able to generate some reverberations among the ranks of the schismatic Old Catholics.[25] But the Gallican advocacy of the Conciliar position was persistently discredited in theological circles by the degree to which that position was being prostituted to purely political ends, to the current needs of royal policy or to the persistent drive of the modern state towards jurisdictional omnicompetence within its territorial limits. It was the fate of the Conciliar theory to have been reduced in stature from a strategic weapon of supranational range to a merely tactical device, lodged in the armory of Gallican pretensions and divorced, therefore, from programs of more complex provenance and more exalted purpose. And, as such, it became understandably difficult for theologians to take it seriously as a credible ecclesiological option.

(d) Conciliar Theory and Secular Political Thinking

It is the paradox of the piece of history which we have just outlined, and the tragedy of the Conciliarist ecclesiology, that the very theory which stressed in face of the absolutist demands of the papal monarchy the inherent authority of the community of the faithful, should itself have been bent ultimately to serve the ends of another absolutism that was no less deplorable for being

24. See Oakley, *Political Thought of Pierre d'Ailly,* pp. 214 ff.
25. See Pontien Polman, "Historical Background of Old Catholicism," *Concilium* (Glen Rock, New Jersey, 1965), VII, pp. 159-167.

secular rather than ecclesiastical in nature. And yet the story of the strict Conciliar theory would be incomplete if one limited oneself to tracing its career in Catholic Europe. For in the sixteenth and seventeenth centuries it played a most important constitutionalist role in the Protestant world—though in the context, this time, not of ecclesiology but of secular political theory.[26]

Almost sixty years ago, the English historian John Neville Figgis drew attention to the importance of this new role. And if he was not the first to have done so, the sweep and vigor of his statement contrived, nevertheless, to make it a classic and influential one. The Conciliar movement, he argued, was "the culmination of medieval constitutionalism. It forms the watershed between the medieval and the modern world." And why is this so? Because, in the first place, the scandal of the Great Schism had had the effect of turning attention from the old familiar dispute between the two powers, temporal and spiritual, and focusing it upon the nature of the Church itself. Because, in the second, "speculation on the possible power of the council, as the true depositary of sovereignty within the Church" led them "to treat the Church definitely as one of a class, political societies." Because, in the third, the Conciliar theorists of Constance

appear to have discerned more clearly than their predecessors the meaning of the constitutional experiments which the last two centuries had seen in considerable profusion, to have thought out the principles that underlay them, and based them upon reasoning that applied to all political societies. . . . In a word, they raised the constitutionalism of the past three centuries to a higher power, expressed it in a more universal form, and justified it on grounds of reason, policy and Scripture.[27]

26. The following account is based on my *Political Thought of Pierre d'Ailly*, pp. 218 ff., and my "From Constance to 1688 revisited," *Journal of the History of Ideas*, XXVII (1966), 429-432.
27. Figgis, *Political Thought from Gerson to Grotius: Seven Studies* (New York, 1960), pp. 41–70.

According to Figgis, then, the Conciliar movement, precisely because its principles were expressed "in a form in which they could readily be applied to politics," is to be regarded as "having helped forward modern constitutional tendencies." Thus "even Huguenot writers like DuPlessis Mornay", he said, "were not ashamed of using the doctrine of the Council's superiority over the Pope to prove their own doctrine of the supremacy of the estates over the King." So that, as H. J. Laski put it later on, "the road from Constance" to the Glorious Revolution of 1688 in England was therefore, "a direct one." [28]

Despite the scanty nature of the evidence with which he buttressed his contentions, subsequent scholarship has been kind to Figgis and there has, of late, been a modest accumulation of evidence suggesting very strongly that if he was somewhat off the mark in his assumptions about the source of Conciliar theory he was very much to the point in his claims for its subsequent influence on sixteenth- and seventeenth-century constitutionalist thinking. It is presumably the convocation of Pisa and the renewed circulation of Conciliarist literature occasioned thereby that explains the ease with which constitutionalists and advocates of active resistance against tyrants later on in the century made use of Conciliar arguments in their own discussions of secular politics. A student of Conciliar theory may properly be forgiven if he finds much that is maddeningly familiar in the arguments of Catholic resistance theorists of the Counter Reformation era in France and England, even though an overt acknowledgment of dependence on Conciliar ideas is rare. Writing in the wake of the Protestant Reformation these men were understandably reluctant to make any such acknowledgment. But no such problems plagued the Protestant advocates of resistance theories. In four important works, three of which exerted an immense influence on the political thinking of seventeenth-century England, there is

28. "Political Theory in the Later Middle Ages," *Cambridge Medieval History* (Cambridge, 1911 ff.), VIII, p. 638.

clear evidence of dependence upon Conciliar political ideas. The *De jure magistratuum* usually ascribed to Theodore Beza was explicit enough on these matters for the English royalist, David Owen, to describe it in 1610 as a book "wherein it is said that the people have the same right to depose Kings that are tyrants, which a generall counsell hath to displace a Pope that is a Heretique." [29] A much lengthier appeal to Conciliar theory and practice occurs in the *Shorte Treatise of Politicke Power* written in 1556 during the reign of "Bloody Mary" by John Ponet, exiled Anglican Bishop of Winchester, who reveals a clear grasp of the history of the fifteenth-century councils and of the principles of Conciliar theory, which, interestingly enough, he ascribes to "the canonistes (the pope's own champions)". After considerable elaboration, he draws the familiar conclusion that

if it be lawful for the body of the churche to depose and punishe a Pope . . . how muche the more by the like argumentes, reasones and authoritie, maie Emperours, Kings, princes and other governours, abusing their office, be deposed and removed out of their places and offices, bi the body or state of the Realme or commonwealthe. [30]

Similarly forthright appeals occur also in what were probably the most important and influential of all the political tracts opposing absolute monarchy to appear in the two centuries preceding the publication of Locke's *Second Treatise*—the *De jure regni apud Scotos* of George Buchanan (himself in his earlier Catholic days an adherent of the Conciliar position), and the *Vindiciae contra tyrannos*—a work currently attributed, at least in part,

29. David Owen, *Herod and Pilate Reconciled* (London, 1663), p. 43. The work had previously appeared in 1610 and 1642 under the title of *A persuasion to loyalty*. The French version of the *De jure magistratuum* (*Du droit des magistrats sur les sujets*) is to be found in *Mémoires de l'Estat de France sous Charles IX*, ed. Simon Goulart (Meidelbourg, 1577), II, pp. 735-790; see esp. p. 777.

30. *A Shorte Treatise* (Strassburg, 1556); facsimile edition in W. S. Hudson, *John Ponet (1516-1556): Advocate of Limited Monarchy* (Chicago, 1942), [103]–[105].

to the Huguenot, Philippe du Plessis Mornay. If, says the author of the latter,

> according to the opinions of most of the learned, by decrees of Councils, and by custom on like occasions, it plainly appears that the Council may depose a Pope, who notwithstanding vaunts himself to be the King of Kings, and as much in Dignity above the Emperour, as the Sun is above the Moon . . . [then] . . . who will make any doubt or question, that the general Assembly of the Estates of any Kingdom, who are the representative body thereof, may not only degrade and disthronize and depose a King, whose weakness or folly, is hurtful or pernicious to the State.[31]

It was in the seventeenth century that the influence of these tracts was most strongly felt—and then most notably in England. But English constitutional and political theorists were not wholly dependent upon these resistance theorists of the previous century for an appreciation of the relevance of the Conciliar position to the world of secular politics. Such works as Foxe's *Book of Martyrs* and John White's *Way to the True Church* (1608) also served as bridges to the Conciliarist past—as several passages in William Prynne's *Soveraigne Power of Parliaments and Kingdoms* reveal. Again, Edmond Richer's inclusion of Conciliar tracts by d'Ailly, Major and Almain in his 1606 edition of the complete works of Gerson made conveniently available a whole arsenal of Conciliarist arguments. This arsenal was put to good use during the controversy occasioned in the wake of the Gunpowder plot by the imposition of the Oath of Allegiance upon English Roman Catholics, and it would be proper, indeed, to speak of a veritable reception of Conciliar theory in England at this time. The arguments of men like the Archpriest Blackwell, of Warmington and Widdrington, of Robert Burhill, indeed, of James I himself—these must have done much to direct the attention of Englishmen to the relevant tracts of the Parisian Conciliarists.

31. *Vindiciae contra tyrannos . . . Being a Treatise Written in French and Latin, and Translated out of Both into English* (London, 1689), p. 142.

It is hardly surprising, then, that during the early years of the Civil War, when the opponents of Charles I still pursued the moderate goal of lawful resistance, some of them should choose to cite the Conciliarists and to invoke the Conciliar analogy in much the same way as had their more distinguished sixteenth-century predecessors. Nor is it surprising that the efforts of some of their royalist adversaries should have been deflected into attempts to meet those arguments. On this matter, while it might be forcing the evidence a little to speak, as did Laski, of a direct road from Constance to 1688, it would be hard to deny the existence at least of a path from Constance to 1644.

The conclusion which imposes itself at the end of this survey of the career of Conciliar theory is that that theory was indeed neither as recent and revolutionary in its origins nor as rapid in its demise as most of us tend still to assume. The aftermath of the Conciliar movement involved more than the recovery of papal power, the growth of national state churches, the dashing of reformist and Conciliarist hopes. In matters ecclesiological, the legacy of Conciliar theory was a vital and enduring one and might well have had a greater impact on the constitution of the Church had it not ultimately been discredited by the secular causes it was being used to serve, causes inimical to the interests of an international Church pressed hard by the mounting claims of the national state. In matters political, however, that legacy remained faithful to its origins, and the role it played in the rise of modern forms of limited government should serve to remind us of the true thrust of Conciliar thinking in the classical era. For, as Bishop Ponet reminded his contemporaries during the brief but bloodstained period of papal restoration in England, "By this lawe and argumentes of the Canonistes and example of deprivation of a Pope, are all clokes (wherewith Popes, bishoppes, priestes, kaisers and kinges use to defende their iniquitie) utterly taken awaie." [32]

32. *A Shorte Treatise,* ed. Hudson, [105].

PART II

Ecclesiological

CHAPTER 4

Conciliarism Today

(a) Revival: de Vooght and Küng

Five years ago, Joseph Gill, Professor at the Pontifical Oriental Institute at Rome, gloomily concluded that the "principle of superiority of council over pope, forgotten and denied in the intervening centuries [since Constance], is being revived."[1] Not content with sounding the tocsin he was at pains to stress the difficulties confronting what he called "the conciliarist of today". But the only candidate he nominated for this forbidding title was the Belgian Benedictine, Paul de Vooght, and while in one sense that nomination was entirely appropriate, in another it was somewhat unfortunate. Appropriate because de Vooght was certainly the first to have focussed attention, once more, on the question of the dogmatic status of *Haec sancta*. Unfortunate because to have done this is not necessarily to have merited the title of "conciliarist"—a title which, as we have seen, can be taken to cover a wide and varied range of ideological commitment.

De Vooght began his discussion of the issue in an article which appeared in 1960. Having encountered some initial criticism, he proceeded in subsequent articles to refine and extend his argument, restating the whole case, finally, in a book published in 1965.[2] In his initial statement he restricted himself almost en-

1. "The Fifth Session of the Council of Constance," *Heythrop Journal,* V (1964), 131.
2. "Le Conciliarisme aux conciles de Constance et de Bâle," in B. Botte *et al., Le Concile et les Conciles: Contribution à l'histoire de la vie conciliare de l'église* (Chevetogne-Paris, 1960), pp. 143-181; "Le Conciliarisme aux conciles de Constance et de Bâle (Compléments et précisions)," *Irénikon,* XXXVI (1963), 61-75; "Le concile oecumenique de Constance et le con-

tirely to the role of historian and hesitated to draw any precise theological conclusions. And if his reserve has since melted somewhat, he is still by no means radical in the claims he permits himself to make.

He is careful, right at the outset, to distinguish the moderate Conciliarism of the fathers of Constance from the radical version espoused by Marsilius of Padua. The fathers, he says, did not deny the divine foundation of the Roman primacy. Nor did they usually question the thesis that the Roman church of pope and cardinals was head of the churches and principal authority within the universal Church. But the majority of them were Conciliarist in sympathies. That is to say, the majority of them denied that the authority of the pope or of the Apostolic See was without limits, and affirmed that the general council representing the universal Church possessed the authority to enforce those limits. Thus in certain cases, such as that of an heretical, scandalous or schismatic pope, it possessed by divine right the necessary power to intervene and take whatever measures were necessary to prevent the destruction of the Church—even if such measures extended to the judgment and deposition of popes.

This is the view, de Vooght goes on to argue, that found formal expression in the decree *Haec sancta*, itself no merely emergency measure relevant only to the activity of the Council of Constance, but a doctrinal definition concerning the competence

---

ciliarisme," *Istina,* IX (1963), 57-86; "Le Cardinal Cesarini et le Concile de Constance," in A. Franzen and W. Müller, *Das Konzil von Konstanz: Beiträge zu seiner Geschichte und Theologie* (Freiburg, 1964), pp. 357-381. I base this analysis on the final restatement of his argument in the book *Les pouvoirs du Concile et l'autorité du pape au Concile de Constance* (Paris, 1965). Note that in his first article, while de Vooght argued that *Haec sancta* fulfilled all the requirements necessary to make it a dogmatic decree —including the possession of papal approbation, he did not conclude, nevertheless, that it was dogmatically valid, but restricted himself, instead, to noting the relevance of the whole case to the strict limitations imposed by Vatican I on the exercise of the papal infallibility. Only after the appearance of Hans Küng's book did he draw the obvious conclusion from his own historical arguments.

of all general councils in matters concerning the faith, unity and reform of the Church. Hence the later provision in *Frequens* for regular councils to exercise the control function envisaged. The decree *Haec sancta* was the end-product of a long doctrinal development, it "incontestably reflected the opinion of an imposing majority of fathers and theologians present at the council" (p. 36), and the doctrine it affirmed continued to be a commonplace among theologians and canonists well into the fifteenth century —even among those who, like Cesarini or Nicholas of Cusa, ended by siding with Eugenius IV against the rump Council of Basel. For the radical majority at Basel gave the decree an extended meaning that their predecessors at Constance had not intended, and used it to justify Conciliar interference in the day-to-day government of the Church. As a result, after the dissolution of Basel the decree came increasingly to be regarded as a *faux-pas* about which the less that was said the better.

But despite its abuse and radicalization at the hands of Basel, *Haec sancta* can bear, de Vooght insists, a perfectly orthodox sense and one rooted in the tradition of the Church. He points out that in speaking of the relationship between pope and council it did not use the ambiguous terms "superiority" and "inferiority" that were so to be abused at Basel. It affirmed nothing that diminished *necessarily* the universal jurisdiction of the pope, or his supreme power of convoking councils, or of confirming or approving their decisions. It imposed nothing on the pope and exacted nothing of him—so long, that is, as he did not deviate from the orthodox faith, destroy the unity of the Church or lead it to its destruction.

This being so, it is not surprising that both Martin V and Eugenius IV approved the decree. More than once de Vooght insists that this matter of papal approval is strictly a secondary consideration, but he devotes a great deal of effort, nevertheless, to establishing that both pontiffs did in fact give it, if not their solemn ratification, at least their assent. Martin V, though intent on reasserting papal prerogatives, certainly did not become pope as "the declared adversary" of the Conciliar powers as defined in 1415. He always affirmed the ecumenicity of Constance, and, in so doing, did not distinguish one session or phase from another. He clearly felt himself bound by the norms of *Frequens.* If, in 1418, he toyed with the idea of prohibiting appeals from the pope to a future general council, he backed down, it seems under pressure from Gerson, and never published the prohibition. On February 22 of the same year, in the bull *Inter cunctas,* he demanded submission to the decisions of Constance on matters "in favor of faith and for the good of souls" specifically including the condemnation of Wycliffite and Hussite ideas. At the closing session of the council he declared himself to accept and approve everything that the council had decided "in a conciliar manner on matters of faith".

None of this amounts to a solemn proclamation ratifying the decrees of the council. Nobody at the time, however, demanded such a ratification. But the Council of Basel later on came close to doing so when it demanded of Eugenius IV that he withdraw his bulls dissolving that council and declaring its decrees and statutes null and void. For Basel had solemnly reaffirmed the decrees of Constance on the powers of the council, and Eugenius at first refused to comply because, as he himself pointed out, "his approbation . . . would signify that he admitted the superiority of the council to the pope" (p. 87). And yet in the bull *Dudum sacrum* he finally gave that approbation and in terms general and unqualified enough to satisfy a council composed of men who were already beginning to give the decrees of Constance an extended and radical meaning. Later on, it is true, in the bulls *Moyses vir Dei* (1439) and *Etsi non dubitemus* (1441), he cast doubt on the legitimacy of *Haec sancta,* but de Vooght characterizes the arguments contained in these documents as "confused" and "incoherent". He notes, too, that at the end of his life Eugenius himself seems to have abandoned them, since he admitted formally in 1447 that the general Council of Constance, the decree *Frequens* and all its decrees "belong to the same rank as the other general councils" (pp. 100–101).

Of papal approbations, then, there were more than enough. Indeed, how could they be wanting when, as Cesarini pointed out to Eugenius, the very legitimacy of his papal title and that of Martin V depended on the validity of *Haec sancta* and of the action which Constance had taken on the basis of the doctrinal position defined therein. In any case, because of the context, de Vooght goes on, the matter of papal approbation is a purely secondary issue. Constance was an ecumenical council from the start because it held the supreme power in virtue of which it rid the Church of the rival claimants to the papacy and elected Martin V pope. Given this situation, the decree *Haec sancta* fulfilled all the conditions necessary to make it a dogmatic decree. As such, understood "in its authentic sense" it binds in faith. Conclusion: "There is no longer today any motive for maintaining the [traditional] ostracism of a dogmatic decree which clarifies and confirms a point of doctrine always admitted in the Church and always taught in the schools" (p. 198).

De Vooght's arguments, clearly and forcefully presented, evoked an immediate and equally forceful response—both positive and negative. The clearest and most vigorous of the positive reactions came from Hans Küng in 1962 in the first of his two important ecclesiological works—*Structures of the Church*.[3] Pointing out that "the (traditionally understood) legitimacy of Martin V and all other subsequent popes up to the present day depends on the legitimacy of the Council of Constance and its procedure in the question of the popes" (p. 270), and noting that modern theologians, nevertheless, have not shrunk "from pointing out the non-binding character of the Constance decrees, often

3. *Strukturen der Kirche* (Freiburg, 1962); translated into English by Salvatore Attanasio as *Structures of the Church* (New York, 1964). See ch. 7 and esp. pp. 268-319. The references below are given to this edition.

with quite extraordinary, ostensibly historical arguments", Küng goes on to summarize the findings of "the most recent research in Church history", including de Vooght's important article of 1960. Among those findings he includes (and endorses) the evidence in favor of Martin V's approbation of the Constance decrees—both in his remarks at the closing session of the council and in the bull *Inter cunctas.* Speaking of the latter, he adds:

To be sure . . . it has nothing to do with a formal papal approbation; this Council had expected such approbation as little as had the ecumenical councils of Christian antiquity. This says as little against the binding character of the decrees of the old councils as it does against the binding character of the decrees of Constance. In Nicea as in Constance a general understanding of the Roman bishops, without which no consensus of the Church is possible, altogether sufficed for endowing decrees with a binding character. [Pp. 277–78.]

Thus if Küng is somewhat less concerned with this question of papal approbation and argues that it is not "to be posed anachronistically", he is even more insistent than de Vooght that "the binding character of the decrees of Constance is not to be evaded".[4] *Haec sancta* and *Frequens* were not "something accidental or external, thrust upon the Church from the outside" but "a logical culmination of ideas that were imbedded in the law and doctrine of the Church itself" (pp. 301–302). What was defined was not a "conciliar parliamentarianism" or "radical conciliarism" in accordance with which "the regular lawful administration of the Church should be transferred from the pope to the Council and the pope reduced to a subordinate executive organ of the conciliar parliament" (pp. 284–85). Instead, "what was defined was a distinct kind of superiority of the council (along the lines of . . . moderate 'conciliar theory'), according to which an ecumenical council has the function of a 'control authority', not only in connection with the emergency situation of that time but also for the future on the premise that a possible

4. *Structures,* p. 284.

110

future pope might again lapse into heresy, schism or the like" (p. 285). Conclusion? That "the Church might have been able to avoid many misfortunes after the Council of Constance had the fundamental position of the Constance Council—papal primacy *and* a definite 'conciliar control' been upheld" (p. 285).

(b) Rejection: Gill

If Küng regards the question of papal approbation as peripheral to the dogmatic status of *Haec sancta,* Joseph Gill, perhaps the most vigorous opponent of the point of view he represents, does not.[5] For him, indeed, it is the heart of the matter, perhaps, even, the whole question. What *is* peripheral is the fact (which he is quite willing to admit) that *Haec sancta* was "the logical outcome of the thought and action of the previous years and represented the views of most of the Fathers at Constance" (p. 132). For Constance, he insists, was not, in its early stages when the decree was promulgated, an ecumenical council at all. How could it be? Was it not summoned by an "anti-pope", John XXIII, the creature of the earlier assembly at Pisa which had taken it upon itself to depose two "popes" and which "is not numbered in the list of ecumenical councils generally recognized by the Church" (p. 134). Only if Martin V had been able and willing by "a kind of *sanatio in radice* to make a resolution of a non-conciliar gathering into a conciliar and binding decree" could *Haec sancta* have become dogmatically valid and binding. Whether Martin V would have been *able* to do such a thing, Gill does not presume to decide. But that Martin V did not in fact do so, he is quite willing to affirm. And, in fact, by far the greater part of his article is devoted to a rebuttal of any claim that Martin V or

5. "The fifth session of the Council of Constance," *Heythrop Journal,* V (1964), 131-143. The references below are given to this article. Gill has recently returned to this topic in a more general statement which reveals no change in his position, "Il decreto *Haec sancta synodus* del concilio di Constanza," *Rivista di storia della Chiesa in Italia,* XII (1967), 123-130.

Eugenius IV, either by word or deed, gave their approval to *Haec sancta.*

Thus he points out the spontaneous and unpremeditated character of Martin V's statement during the last session of Constance to the effect that he approved whatever the council had done "in a conciliar manner on matters of faith", and lays great stress on the fact that the Conciliarists of Basel, in reaffirming the teaching contained in *Haec sancta,* never made anything of Martin's alleged approbation. Again, if "the argument from *Inter cunctas* is a more serious one", it is serious not because it refers to Constance as "a general council" but because it does not "distinguish stages in the council" and refers to one event, the condemnation of Wyclif, "dating from before Gregory's convocation of the council (after which date one need not hesitate to call it a general council)" (pp. 135–136). Nevertheless, even if Martin could in good conscience "refer to the gathering in all its stages as a general council representing the universal Church", it does not necessarily follow

that he had to hold that everything that that council declared was automatically infallible and binding on the universal Church. He could hold that its enactments still needed papal approbation before being conciliar decrees in the fullest sense. [P. 136.]

Thus, approving the condemnations of Wyclif and Hus, he could regard them, therefore, and describe them in *Inter cunctas* as "official decisions of the ecumenical council". But he certainly did not approve *Haec sancta* "in set terms", and "almost certainly" did not even approve it indirectly.

Similarly with respect to the attitude of Eugenius IV Gill admits that Eugenius said "nothing direct . . . to diminish the status of the Council of Constance" (p. 138). He points out, however, that in *Moyses vir Dei* and *Etsi non dubitemus* he certainly impugned the ecumenicity of the fifth session when *Haec sancta* was promulgated. What, then, of *Dudum sacrum?*

Merely, he says, Eugenius's formal declaration of adherence to the Council of Basel. Nowhere in it "did he give formal approval to its decrees either *en bloc* or individually" (p. 142). Had the fathers of Basel thought that the bull was an admission of Eugenius's adhesion to the Conciliar principles of *Haec sancta* they would surely have used it more often than they did in their later polemics against him.

As for the remarks Eugenius made in 1447, they were "most eloquently reticent" (p. 140) in that while they include a reference to *Frequens* they "carefully" exclude any mention of *Haec sancta.* Eugenius's real views "on where lay the supreme authority in the Church were solemnly expressed in the decree of union with the Greeks".[6] Conclusion? "Historically it may not be asserted that the fifth session of the Council of Constance was certainly a session of an ecumenical council or that either Martin V or Eugenius IV by a subsequent approval made the decision of that session ecumenical and binding on the Church" (pp. 142–143).

(c) Mediation: Jedin and Franzen

Given these diametrically opposed positions the temptation, of course, is to try to seek middleground between the two extremes, and some scholars—notably Hubert Jedin and August Franzen —have tried to do precisely that.

Jedin's treatment of this question first appeared in 1962. He discusses the contributions of de Vooght and Küng only in footnotes and in a postscript. Gill he mentions not at all.[7] In delineat-

6. "The fifth session," 143; for the decree of union, see above, ch. 3, pp. 83-84.

7. *Bischöfliches Konzil oder Kirchenparlament? Ein Beitrag zur Ekklesiologie der Konzilien von Konstanz und Basel,* Vorträge der Aeneas Silvius Stiftung an der Universität Basel, II (2nd. ed.; Basel u. Stuttgart, 1965). In the second edition, to which all references below are given, Jedin adds to the postscript (pp. 38-39), a few further remarks on relevant works which appeared between 1962 and 1965.

ing his position, however, it will be helpful to relate it to the positions of all three of these men. Thus, on the one hand, he is closer to Gill than to de Vooght on the question of papal approbation. Despite the awkward position in which they found themselves (since the legitimacy of their titles depended on the action taken at Constance), he finds no evidence that Martin V and his successor pronounced themselves "to be agreed upon the universal and absolute validity of the decree *Haec sancta*" or that they "formally confirmed" it (p. 17). On the other hand, he is clearly with Küng in his desire to avoid posing anachronistically this question of papal approbation. Unlike Trent, he notes, Constance did not seek papal confirmation for its decrees or deem it necessary. And, in any case, the history of the councils makes it very clear that the form of papal concurrence in conciliar enactments has undergone considerable change over the course of time.

Jedin is with Küng and de Vooght, again, in his insistence that *Haec sancta* preserves a genuine ecclesiastical tradition, but perhaps closer to Gill when he finally makes clear what he takes that tradition to involve. Thus he can see no objection to the decree's initial assertion that the general council represented the Catholic Church. But the second assertion that it held its power immediately from Christ, he sees as being more difficult to defend. Citing Ratzinger, he says it is via the episcopal college in unity with the pope that power is mediated to the council and pope and college should not be set in opposition one to another. Given this position, it is not too surprising that he believes that the decree's third assertion, which subjected pope to council in certain cases, simply cannot be taken at its face value.

In the first place, the historical circumstances surrounding it must be taken into account, and, when they are, the range of its claims is notably reduced. John XXIII, against whom it was directed, was no indisputably legitimate pope since there were still two other papal claimants. And "this circumstance", Jedin says, "is in my judgment decisive." Why? Because "in the light

114

of the definitions of the First Vatican Council only the undoubtedly legitimate successor of Peter is endowed with infallibility
and with the pastoral power over the whole Church" (p. 11).
In the absence of such a successor, then, the type of emergency
situation arises in which the canonists had insisted that the interest of the whole Church must come before that of the pope. Confronted in aggravated form with such an emergency situation,
the fathers of Constance framed *Haec sancta*. It is, therefore, no
"universal, as it were, free-floating definition of belief" but
rather "an emergency measure to meet a quite definite exceptional
case" (p. 12).

In the second place, the reference later on in the decree to
the necessity (backed by sanctions) for papal obedience to the
mandates of "this holy synod" or of "any other legitimately
assembled council in the matters aforesaid" should not be taken,
as de Vooght and Küng have taken it, to contradict this interpretation of the decree as a limited and extraordinary emergency
measure. To do this is to overlook the fact that "the sanction can
in no case reach further than the law". The clause in question
must refer to the possibility that the settlement of the schism
might occur, not at Constance, but at "another" general council,
which would still be confronted, therefore, with the extraordinary
emergency situation which *Haec sancta* was framed to meet (p.
32, n. 24; pp. 38–39). The same point is relevant to the renewal
of the decree in 1432 and 1434 at Basel. On both of those occasions the council was confronted with a situation comparable to
that of Constance in 1415. On both occasions Eugenius had
ordered the dissolution of the council and it was faced, as a result,
with the necessity of securing its own existence. Only in 1439,
after the final breach with Eugenius, does a change take place in
the circumstances and an escalation occur in the claims being
made for the decree. Only then, when it was attempting to depose an unquestionably legitimate pope, did the council accord
an absolute dogmatic value to *Haec sancta* and try to impose the
superiority of council to pope as a truth of the faith. But this was

115

the work of a mere rump-council intent on turning itself, in a manner wholly alien to the Conciliar tradition, into what amounted to a "church parliament" (pp. 13–15).

Jedin admits that his interpretation has its own problems and that they are numerous. But he believes that they are less numerous than those attendant upon Küng's position, and he remains firm in his conclusion that *Haec sancta* does not contain doctrine accepted by an unquestionably legitimate pope and binding in all its parts and for all time (p. 38). August Frazen states himself to be in general agreement with this conclusion.[8] Thus, he is not particularly interested in the matter of papal approbation of *Haec sancta,* and he seems to think, like Jedin, that there was no question of any *formal* papal confirmation of that decree. Again, if "we must hold on to the fact that this decree *Haec sancta* has to count as a valid decree of an ecumenical council" we still have to ask: "What is its theological significance? Can and should it be granted dogmatic validity?" [9]

To the latter question Franzen replies that the council

did not intend the decree *Haec sancta* to be a norm of faith, as none of the participants meant to define an infallible dogma. The decree is not the kind of dogmatic definition which Vatican I describes.[10]

Only because the fathers of Basel reinterpreted the decree in 1439 "in a radical conciliarist sense" was it taken to be a dogmatic statement. Only because of this did Constance get "the

8. The most recent statement of his position is contained in his article, "The Council of Constance: Present State of the Problem," *Concilium* (Glen Rock, New Jersey, 1965), VII, pp. 29-68, esp. at pp. 45-68. This lengthy article is largely dependent upon two earlier articles of his: "Zur Vorgeschichte des Konstanzer Konzils Vom Ausbruch des Schismas bis zum Pisanum" and "Das Konzil der Einheit: Einigung bemühungen und konziliare Gedanken auf dem Konstanzer Konzil. Die Dekrete 'Haec sancta' und 'Frequens'," in *Das Konzil von Konstanz,* ed. Franzen and Müller, pp. 3-35, 69-112.

9. "Council of Constance," 57.

10. "Council of Constance," 59; "Das Konzil von Einheit," 103-104.

reputation of having defined the superiority of the council over the papacy and of having laid down a basic law for the church's organization".[11] But what, then, is the precise significance of the decree? It was a measure for emergencies, a piece of legislation designed to give legal force to the traditional canonistic teaching that a general council was superior in authority to an heretical pope who by lapsing into heresy had ceased *ipso facto* to be pope. The council "neither proclaimed nor intended to proclaim an irrevocable dogmatic definition". Instead, "it merely incorporated an existing positive law in general law and so turned it from an obscure, controversial canonical regulation into a proper law which could deal with any such cases in the future on a legal basis".[12]

Franzen clearly thinks himself at one with Jedin in this interpretation and he cites the latter approvingly when advancing it. It is important, however, to note two things in particular about his line of argument. In the first place, whereas Jedin had regarded as "decisive" the fact that John XXIII was *not* an undoubtedly legitimate pope and had made this fact central to his interpretation of *Haec sancta,* Franzen argues that John was "a legitimate and generally accepted pope".[13] In the second place (a point which follows from the first), whereas Jedin seems to have regarded *Haec sancta* as designed only for the case of John XXIII and applicable only to a pope the legitimacy of whose title is suspect, and, hence, as a very specific emergency measure, Franzen interprets it as a legal formulation of the old canonist position vis-à-vis the status of popes who, by lapsing into heresy or by fostering schism and becoming, as a result, suspect of heresy, had ceased to be anything more than pseudo-popes and had fallen subject, therefore, to judgment by the Church. If it was an emergency measure, then, it was one de-

11. "Council of Constance," 61.
12. *Ibid.,* 67.
13. *Ibid.,* 43.

117

signed not only for the existing emergency, but for comparable cases in the future. Hence, he can claim that his interpretation of the contents of the decree is identical with that of Küng, though he denies Küng's assertion that the decree is still possessed of dogmatic binding force. In making this claim, however, he is clearly mistaken. He is also mistaken in regarding his interpretation as identical with that of Jedin. The mediating position he has adopted is clearly a new and distinct one. As such it must stand or fall on its own merits.

(d) Judgment

The writers whom I have been discussing are not the only ones to have addressed themselves to this issue.[14] Nor have I attempted to reproduce all the numerous arguments they themselves advance in support of their respective positions. In particular, it should be noted that in the interests of simplification I have made little or no reference to the arguments they ground in their respective interpretations of the decree *Frequens*.[15] But, then, what they make of *Frequens* depends very much on what they believe they can make of *Haec sancta,* and, in selecting some

14. For other contributions ranging from reaffirmations of the traditional Catholic assessment of *Haec sancta* to statements sympathetic with the general approach of Küng and De Vooght, see I. H. Pichler, *Die Verbindlichkeit der Konstanzer Dekrete* (Vienna, 1967), Heinz Hürten, "Zur Ekklesiologie der Konzilien von Konstanz und Basel", *Theologische Revue,* LIX (1963), 361-372, the articles by Hürten, H. Riedlinger, H. Zimmerman and R. Baümer in Franzen and Müller, *Das Konzil von Konstanz,* and by W. Brandmüller in *Römische Quartalschrift,* LXII (1967), and Yves Congar's "Conclusion" to Botte *et al., Le Concile et les Conciles.* Brian Tierney has contributed an essay entitled "Hermeneutics and History: The Problem of *Haec Sancta"* to the forthcoming volume *Essays in Medieval History for Presentation to Bertie Wilkinson,* edited by T. A. Sandquist and Michael R. Powicke (Toronto, 1969). In it he sketches out a position that can perhaps best be described as mediating between those of Jedin and Küng.

15. Thus, e.g., Gill, while admitting that Martin V obeyed *Frequens,* notes that he dared not do otherwise, and that, in any case, the decree was "disciplinary and not doctrinal"—"The fifth session," 138.

principal branches from among the dense foliage of their argumentation, I do not think I have distorted their position. Nor do I believe that by concentrating attention on these writers have I distorted the general picture. For these are the leading figures in the controversy and their arguments are fully representative of the rather narrow range of options open to anyone who wishes to make an independent judgment on the issue.

Despite these disclaimers, however, and despite the selectivity and simplification involved (if not necessarily evident) in the preceding sections of this chapter, the picture which emerges is still so complex and so confusing that the prospect of having to stand in judgment on the several conflicting positions is at first glance a somewhat intimidating one. Not that these writers fail to leave themselves open to criticism. There are innumerable minor points on which one could take issue with them. For example, de Vooght's assertion that the thinking of d'Ailly and Gerson reveals Marsilian influence is a highly questionable one.[16] So, too, the curious assumption of both Gill and Franzen that only decrees that lay claim to infallibility can claim also to possess binding force.[17] Or again, the hesitancy evident in Jedin's logic when he chooses to regard the reaffirmations of *Haec sancta* in 1432 and 1434 as having occurred in circumstances similar to the original crisis of 1415, whereas the reaffirmation of the decree in 1439 was a wholly different matter.[18] Why? Because whereas John XXIII was not an indisputably legitimate pope, Eugenius IV was. But, then, Eugenius was presumably no

16. *Pouvoirs du Concile*, p. 15, n. 1.
17. See above, pp. 112 and 116. The assumption seems even more curious in the light of the strident claims currently being made for the binding force of *Humanae vitae* which does not lay claim to infallibility, and being made, ironically enough, by the same curialist clique which had earlier been willing to argue that the pope was not bound by Vatican II's Pastoral Constitution on the Church in the Modern World. *Casti Connubii*, in its opinion, took precedence to the conciliar document. On this, see the revealing remarks of Bernard Häring, "The Encyclical Crisis," *Commonweal*, September 6, 1968, 588-594.
18. Jedin, *Bischöfliches Konzil oder Kirchenparlament*, p. 13.

119

less legitimate in 1432 and 1434 than he was to be in 1439. At this point Jedin's line of argument is not fully coherent, and it is this fuzziness that opens the way, in turn, to Franzen's misinterpretations.

These are not to be dismissed lightly. If one were to probe somewhat more deeply one would have to raise several objections about the way in which he handles not only the matters at issue, but also the primary and secondary authorities to which he turns for help. Thus, his failure to take cognizance of Tierney's stress on the contribution to the Conciliar theory of late medieval Decretalist corporative thinking, and (a related point), his concern to restrict the title of "Conciliarist" to close followers of Marsilius of Padua and to deny it to such advocates of the strict Conciliar theory as Gerson and d'Ailly, serve only to introduce further confusion into what is already a rather clouded picture.[19] Similarly, if he really thinks his interpretation of the contents of *Haec sancta* can be identical both with that of Küng and that of Jedin, he has either misread the works of those men or has not himself succeeded in saying what he wants to say. In either case, he would be well advised to re-read with attention both their works and his own.

But it is only when one examines the way in which some of these writers handle the question of papal approbation that one gets at all close to the heart of the problem. In his first article, though de Vooght admitted that the type of approbation allegedly given to *Haec sancta* by Martin V and Eugenius IV did not possess the solemn character required by the First Vatican Council for *ex cathedra* statements, he does seem to place more stress on this approbation than the historical evidence permits,[20] and this tendency is still somewhat evident in his book. On the other hand, Jedin dismisses the possibility of a genuine papal approbation perhaps a little too lightly. On this issue, Küng's assessment

19. "Council of Constance," 40 ff.
20. "Le conciliarisme à Constance et à Bâle," esp. pp. 180-181.

is doubtless the most balanced, but the more important point, surely, is that Küng, Jedin, de Vooght—all three of them—are ultimately willing to agree that the matter at least of a *formal* papal approbation is strictly a secondary question.

For Gill, however, it is the big question, and he is the less convincing because of his comparative isolation on the matter. Moreover, given the subtlety with which Conciliarists like Zabarella or Gerson or d'Ailly handle the question of the location of the *plenitudo potestatis*, I must confess myself bemused at Gill's bland assumption that the definition of papal primacy contained in the Florentine decree of union with the Greeks excluded henceforth the very possibility of even the remotest sympathy with the strict Conciliar theory on the part of anyone who aspired to be orthodox. Nor do I find at all convincing the case against papal approbation which he builds upon the silence of Martin V and Eugenius IV on that specific decree. This is particularly true of the way in which he handles the remarks Eugenius made in 1447.[21] Indeed, this last maneuver, with its unsupported attribution to Eugenius of an "eloquent reticence" and a "careful" exclusion, strikes me as nothing less than the product of exegetical desperation.

This last remark is intended in full seriousness and it may serve to open the way through the jungle of assertion and counter-assertion to a clear judgment on this crucial question of the dogmatic status of *Haec sancta.* When Küng's book appeared, de Vooght commented, and with justice, that no contemporary theologian had before admitted the validity of the Constance definition of the superiority of council to pope. "It is without doubt the first time in contemporary Catholic theology that a theologian has loyally accepted these incontestable historical data and tried to interpret them." [22] This may be surprising enough,

21. See above, p. 113.
22. "Le conciliarisme aux conciles de Constance et de Bâle (Compléments et précisions)," *Irénikon,* XXXVI (1963), 74-75.

but less surprising, surely, than the fact that so very few Catholic *historians* have been willing to accept these data. In this respect, a perusal of the standard modern Catholic encyclopedias is most revealing.

Thus, whereas in 1908 the article on "Councils, General" in the *Catholic Encyclopedia* omitted Pisa from the list of ecumenical councils, declared Constance to be legitimate "when Gregory XII had formally convoked it" and Basel to be ecumenical only "till the end of the twenty-fifth session," [23] in 1911 the comparable article in the *Dictionnaire de théologie catholique* did not include Pisa, Constance or Basel at all in its list of ecumenical councils, but jumped from Vienne (1311–12) to Florence (1339–45)! [24] At the same time, elsewhere in the *Dictionnaire,* Baudrillart noted that nobody doubted the ecumenicity of Constance from the moment of Martin V's election and that more and more were coming to push the critical moment back to the time of Gregory XII's convocation of the council.[25] Similarly, elsewhere in the *Catholic Encyclopedia,* Salembier concluded that "perhaps it is wise to say with Bellarmine that the [Pisan] assembly was a general council which is neither approved nor disapproved." [26]

Over fifty years later, Vincke, in the second edition of the *Lexikon für Theologie und Kirche* insisted that the question of the ecumenicity of Pisa had never been finally settled, and Fink, in the same work, argued that a specific papal confirmation of Constance did not enter into the question and that it would not do, historically speaking, to judge ecumenical only the last few sessions under Martin V.[27] Nevertheless, in the *New Catholic Encyclopedia,* published shortly afterwards (1967), while Tier-

23. *Catholic Encyclopedia,* s.v. "Councils, General."
24. *Dict. de théol. cath.,* s.v., "Conciles."
25. *Dict. de théol. cath.,* s.v. "Constance (Concile de)."
26. *Cath. Encycl.,* s.v. "Pisa."
27. *Lex für Theol. u. Kirche,* s.v. "Pisa (4. Synoden)," and s.v. "Konstanz (3. Konzil)."

ney is very cautious in his handling of the question of the ecumenicity of Constance (concluding, in a rather gingerly fashion, that Constance was "an assembly of ecclesiastical notables who probably did not constitute a validly convoked council at the time of the enactment [of *Haec sancta*]"),[28] Pisa is definitely excluded from the list of ecumenical councils given in another article.[29] Indeed, L. E. Boyle states flatly: "Since the Council of Pisa was not convoked by papal authority, it is not recognized by the Church as ecumenical," and goes on to venture the extraordinary comment that what it did ended by making imperative "the solution adopted at the Council of Constance in 1415, when the three contending popes *were persuaded to retire*" (italics mine).[30]

A similar incoherence and confusion may be remarked in the varying judgments passed in these encyclopedias on the legitimacy of the rival lines of contending popes during the period of the Great Schism. Thus in the *Catholic Encyclopedia* the Avignonese claimants are treated consistently as anti-popes, but while the Pisan pontiffs are included in the list of legitimate popes, the individual article on Alexander V notes that "canonists and historians of the Schism still discuss" the question of his legitimacy, and that on John XXIII refers to that pope bluntly as an "antipope of the Pisan party".[31]

More revealing, however, is the fact that over the last half-

<hr/>

28. *New Cath. Encycl.*, s.v. "Constance, Council of."

29. *New Cath. Encycl.*, s.v. "Councils, General (History of)."

30. A euphemism surely of breathtaking proportions, see *New Cath. Encycl.*, s.v. "Pisa, Council of." Cf. K. A. Fink, "Zur Beurteilung des Grossen Abendländischen Schismas," *Zeitschrift für Kirchengeschichte*, LXXIII (1962), 337, for other recent lists of councils which exclude Pisa and Basel.

31. See *Cath. Encycl.*, s.v. "Pope," "Alexander V, Pope," and "John XXIII, antipope of the Pisan Party." Similarly, in the *Lexikon für Theologie und Kirche* (2nd ed.), while in one place it is said that no certain decision can be made on the legitimacy of the Avignonese popes and while it is indicated that a strong case can be made for the legitimacy of the Pisan popes, in another Clement VII, Benedict XIII and Alexander V are all described as "antipopes," and in yet another John XXIII as "Konzilspapst" (s.v. "Papstliste," "Alexander V," "Benedikt XIII," "Clemens VII," "Johannes XXIII").

century a certain development is evident in the views expressed on this question of legitimacy. Thus, in 1911, in the *Catholic Encyclopedia,* Salembier could say that "an almost general opinion asserts that both he [Alexander V] and his successor, John XXIII, were true popes".[32] Similarly, in the *Dictionnaire de théologie catholique,* while no clear judgment was passed on the Avignonese pontiffs, Alexander V was treated as a legitimate pope (notice being taken of the fact that his title is contested), and if the legitimacy of John XXIII's claim was questioned, it was because of the suspicion that his election was simoniacal and not because of any doubts about the rectitude of the proceedings at the Council of Pisa.[33] In 1949 and 1952, however, the *Enciclopedia Cattolica* listed all the Avignonese and Pisan pontiffs as "antipopes", and, in 1959, the volume of the *Twentieth Century Encyclopedia of Catholicism* followed suit, stating specifically that "Alexander V of the Council of Pisa cannot be regarded as a legitimate pope".[34] In 1967, the *New Catholic Encyclopedia* concurred, and it did so with a dogmatism tempered only by the recognition that some of the "popes in the period of the Great Schism . . . were only subsequently classified as antipopes",[35] and by Mollat's admission that "the question of the legitimacy of his [John XXIII's] claim to the Papal See is still unanswered". But this last remark occurs, ironically enough, in an article entitled (editorially?): "John XXIII, *Antipope*".[36]

Obviously there is nothing new about the willingness to classify the Avignonese pontiffs as antipopes, but it is only in the last twenty years that that willingness has extended also to the Pisan

32. *Cath. Encycl.,* s.v. "Pisa, Council of."

33. *Dict. de théol. cath.,* s.v. "Alexandre V," Benoit XIII, pape d'Avignon," "Clement VII," "Jean XXIII".

34. *Enciclopedia cattolica,* s.v. "Papa" and "Antipapi" (and they are all listed as "antipapi autentici" as opposed to "antipapi dubbi"; Vladimir d'Ormesson, *The Papacy* (New York, 1959), p. 139 (vol. 81 of *The Twentieth Century Encyclopedia of Catholicism*).

35. *New Cath. Encycl.,* s.v. "Popes, List of"; see also articles s.v. "Clement VII, Antipope," "Benedict XIII, Antipope," "Peter of Candia (Alexander V, Antipope)," "John XXIII, Antipope."

36. Italics mine. *New Cath. Encycl.,* s.v. "John XXIII, Antipope," 1021.

popes, who, earlier on, were widely regarded as legitimate. Given the fact that this development runs counter to a growing tendency among historians to regard the whole question of the legitimacy of the Roman and Avignonese lines of popes as one that cannot be settled *historically*,[37] the suspicion arises that it has no roots in historical scholarship.

This suspicion is, in fact, justified. The development in question reflects a development in what K. A. Fink has called the "curialist opinion", which has long been accustomed to treat the Roman line as the legitimate one and the Avignonese as illegitimate, but which only in 1947 began as a matter of course to downgrade the Pisan pontiffs to the latter category.[38] In that year a new list of popes was published in the *Annuario Pontificio* categorizing the Pisan popes as antipopes and replacing the previous list (published annually from 1913–46) which had treated them as legitimate. The new list was the work of Angelo Mercati, Prefect of the Vatican Archives, and was based on the list included by Duchesne in his famous edition of the *Liber Pontificalis* (1886) and upon the changes introduced in 1904–5 by P. F. Ehrle, the then Prefect of the Vatican Library. Although neither Ehrle nor Mercati made any bones about the fact that their judgment concerning the legitimacy of the popes during the period of the Great Schism was based, not on historical grounds alone but on canonistic and theological criteria as well, Catholic historians do not in general seem to have been disposed to question that judgment and it has passed over into the encyclopedias and textbooks.[39]

The fact of the matter is that "the list of popes in the *Annuario Pontificio* can be regarded to some degree as an official pro-

37. A tendency reflected at least in one of the articles in the second edition of the *Lexikon für Theologie und Kirche,* s.v. "Papstliste" (by Baümer). See above, ch. 1, p. 46.

38. K. A. Fink, "Zur Beurteilung des Grossen Abendländischen Schismas," *Zeitschrift für Kirchengeschichte,* LXXIII (1962), 335-337.

39. Fink, "Beurteilung," 335-336; cf. *Annuario Pontificio* (Città del Vaticano, 1947), and Angelo Mercati, "The New List of Popes," *Mediaeval Studies,* IX (1947), 71-80. This article begins with an introductory essay

nouncement",[40] and the recent trend in the direction of down-grading the status of the Pisan pontiffs to that of "anti-popes" is a striking example of the failure of Catholic historians to view these critical questions relating to the Great Schism in fully historical terms. Indeed, the confusion and disarray evident in these encyclopedia discussions of councils and popes bear eloquent witness to the widespread fear that the historical facts will simply not accord with the high papalist ecclesiological vision that became a commonplace during the years following Vatican I and that is still widespread in the Church at large today.

Such a fear is well-founded. If the legitimacy of John XXIII's title is admitted, then it becomes impossible even in modern canonistic terms to deny that Constance was an ecumenical council right from the start, and well-nigh impossible to impugn the dogmatic validity of *Haec sancta.* If, on the other hand, a definite and certain judgment on the legitimacy of all three lines of papal claimants is admitted to elude our grasp, then, on those same terms, we might be led to question the ecumenicity of Constance, hence the validity of Martin V's election by that council, and hence the validity of all subsequent titles. To get around that difficulty one would have to argue that the Council of Constance

---

(71-72) which had appeared in the *Osservatore Romano* of January 19, 1947. Mercati acknowledges his indebtedness to the work of Duchesne, but adds: "Naturally I have reviewed and controlled everything according to the state of present day historical science." He gives, however, no reason for his reclassification of the Pisan pontiffs as antipopes. Duchesne, himself, had listed them as true pontiffs—see L. Duchesne, *Le Liber Pontificalis* (Paris, 1892), II, p. lxxviii. A new edition of that work appeared without any editorial change on that point—*Le Liber Pontificalis*, Bibliothèque des écoles françaises d'Athènes et de Rome (Paris, 1955), p. lxxviii. Mercati is presumably relying on the unspecified "theological-canonical criteria" which he invokes elsewhere in his listing (p. 76, n. 19).

40. More official, it would seem, than the statement of a pope! When in 1958 the late Pope John XXIII chose his title he announced that the name John had been borne by twenty-two popes *"extra legitimitatis discussiones"*—making it clear, thereby, that he was passing no judgment on the legitimacy of the Pisan line. But this did not accord with the mandates of the *Annuario Pontificio,* and in the later official re-edition of the speech in the *Acta Apostolicae Sedis* the words *"extra legitimitatis discussiones"* are no longer to be found—see Fink, "Beurteilung," 336.

was ecumenical at the time of its ending of the schism and Martin V a legitimate pope precisely because he himself approved the activity of the council retroactively and thus confirmed his own election. But, then, Martin V could not have approved *Haec sancta* unless it were, in fact, already valid. Otherwise, he himself would not have been pope and possessed of the authority to approve it.

Not too persuasive an argument. But neither is the alternative position which seeks to evade all of these dangerous quicksands by insisting that the Roman line was the sole legitimate line and that it was only because Gregory XII convoked Constance before abdicating that the council became ecumenical and Martin V's election accordingly valid.[41] For in that case the numerous cardinals participating in the election of Martin V who belonged to the Avignonese and Pisan obediences would have to be classified as pseudo-cardinals. And if one is so concerned about the proprieties of the canonistic regulation stipulating the need for a papal summons to make a council ecumenical, one should surely be equally concerned about comparable canonistic regulations concerning the legal requirements for a papal election to be a valid one. In any case, this approach, by laying claim to access on this critical issue to a divine viewpoint, privileged and extra-historical, makes a mockery of the anguish felt by countless dedicated churchmen, the majority of whom did not at the time admit the validity of Gregory's claim.

The obvious solution, of course, is to cut through the canonistic barriers, to abandon the obsession with confining the divine activity in the Church to the well-trodden paths of the 1917 *Codex Juris Canonici,* and to insist that, whatever the positive laws, Christ always continued to endow his Church with the authority to prevent its own destruction. But this obvious solution was

41. This approach has to face the further problem that the Church has always regarded as valid the conciliar condemnation of the teachings of Wyclif and Hus. But this occurred in 1415 *before* Gregory's "convocation". Hence, the notion of Martin V's retroactive approval of the earlier activity of the council must perforce enter the picture again.

precisely the solution adopted at the time; it was the Conciliarist solution, and in the wake of Vatican I it has seemed to the vast majority of Catholic scholars—historians and theologians alike —to be a solution irrevocably branded as heterodox. Hence the high degree of uneasiness, confusion, dialectical gymnastic and sheer distortion evident in most Catholic analyses of these sensitive issues.

Only against this background can one really understand the writers discussed in the earlier sections of this chapter. Each one of them stresses the importance of a fully *historical* understanding of the critical events at Constance. But, of them all, it is Küng alone—the theologian and the only non-historian among them— who is really prepared "to take cognizance of historical facts, even if they lie athwart current dogmatic theology and force us to qualify notions to which we were accustomed".[42] In every other case one can detect in what should be purely historical decisions the distorting pressure of modern theological and canonistic norms. This was true even of de Vooght in his initial discussion of the issue. Only after Küng published his interpretation did de Vooght abandon his hesitation and go on to draw what was the obvious conclusion from his own arguments—namely, that *Haec sancta* possessed a continuing dogmatic validity. Similarly with Jedin and Franzen. Jedin lays great stress on the importance of understanding Conciliar decrees in their full historical context. But while he is careful to analyze *Haec sancta* in the context of *events,* he certainly does not interpret it in the context of the ecclesiological thinking of the time—and perhaps with good reason since, as we have seen, the ecclesiology dominant among those who, after all, framed its provisions and voted it through, was Conciliarist. Instead, the perspective in which he prefers to assess the crucial superiority clause is that of "the definitions of Vatican I". And, then, in order to avoid the conclusion that the

---

42. Helmut Riedlinger, "Hermeneutische Uberlegungen zu den Konstanzer Dekreten," in Franzen and Müller, eds., *Das Konzil von Konstanz,* p. 214.

decree was something more than an emergency measure evoked by and geared to the crisis of 1415, he is forced to give so strained an interpretation of the reference to "any other legitimately assembled council", that he himself, under criticism from Hürten, has since had to concede that this interpretation is beset with grave difficulties.[43]

Some comparable distortions are evident in Franzen—notably his insistence on measuring the Conciliar decrees of Constance against Vatican I's criteria for the promulgation of infallible dogmas. But it is Gill, distinguished historian though he is, who is most thoroughly anachronistic. There is a qualitative difference between his position and that of Küng. There is a gulf fixed between them, and it lies between those, on the one hand, who are willing to open themselves to the events of history "even if [those events] lie athwart current dogmatic theology", and those, on the other hand, for whom the Ultramontane ecclesiology of the late-nineteenth century and the ambiguous dispositions of the 1917 *Code,* present themselves with all the force of revelation and are accorded an absolute priority over the untidinesses and inconsistencies of the past.

As an historian, my sympathies can only lie with the former. When Gill affirms, in effect, that the Roman line of claimants to the papacy was the legitimate line, even after Pisa, and that John XXIII was, therefore, nothing more than an antipope, he is pre-empting, for extra-historical reasons, a question that in principle can properly be decided on historical grounds alone and in practice, it seems, cannot be decided at all. When he assumes that the ecumenicity of any general council depends upon its convocation by the pope, and when he denies, as a result, the ecumenicity of Constance before its "convocation" by Gregory XII and the validity of those of its decrees not explicitly approved by Martin V, he is in fact asserting that the agonizing realities of history must give way before the proprieties of

<hr/>

43. Jedin, *Bischöfliches Konzil,* p. 39; the reference is to Hürten, "Zur Ekklesiologie der Konzilien von Konstanz und Basel," 364-365.

canonistic arrangements which, however much they have been honored in modern and (less consistently) in medieval times, can lay no claim to be of anything but human provenance. As a result, even if one is not inclined to suspect the impartiality of his motivation, one can scarcely avoid impugning the historicity of his argumentation. An Ultramontane *theology* may still, conceivably, be defensible. But there is surely no place for an Ultramontane *historiography*.

It is Küng, the theologian, then, who emerges from among these historians as the man most truly willing to take his conciliar and papal history straight.[44] He clearly feels no uneasiness at having to admit that twentieth-century writers are in no better position than fourteenth- and fifteenth-century churchmen when it comes to making a decision about the legitimacy of the rival claimants to the papal office during the schism. Nor is he embarrassed by the fact that some general councils in the past were presumptuous enough to come into existence without papal convocation and untidy enough to have had their decrees accepted by the Church at large as dogmatically valid even without the niceties of formal papal approbation. As a result, he is able to approach the extraordinary situation at Constance with a minimum of theological anxiety and a maximum of intellectual security. And the accuracy of the conclusions he draws, certainly on the question of the dogmatic validity of *Haec sancta,* and, with only one qualification, on the question of the meaning of the decree, is surely borne out by our own analysis of the nature and history of the schism and of Conciliar theory. On this matter it remains only to make a few concluding remarks.

(i) *The question of dogmatic validity:* After Pisa the disagreement about the respective claims of the Roman and Avignonese pontiffs was pushed to one side and by far the greater part of the Church regarded Alexander V, and, after him, John XXIII, as the true pope. If Martin V's title (and that of his successors) is

44. De Vooght, of course, comes a close second.

to be valid, then so, too, has to be the procedure followed by the Council of Constance in disposing of John XXIII. But that procedure was grounded in the claims made in *Haec sancta* for Conciliar authority. And, given the situation, it is gratuitous—ludicrous even—to wrangle about the need for formal papal approbation to make that decree valid. In any case, the claims it made by no means constituted a revolutionary innovation. They were deeply rooted in the tradition of the Church, and, despite papal antipathy, survived for centuries in at least one of the two main traditions of Catholic ecclesiological thinking. Finally, if that papal antipathy is used to prove the lack of any papal approval of *Haec sancta,* it can hardly be used to explain as well the absence of any formal papal repudiation of that same decree —even when some papal sympathizers felt such a repudiation desirable.

(ii) *The meaning of the decree:* If one needs convincing that *Haec sancta* can be read in more than one way, the interpretation given to it by the radical Conciliarists at Basel should suffice to do so. But, as we have seen, the Conciliar "parliamentarianism" of the radicals at Basel, with its programmatic interference in the day to day government of the Church, was not what the moderate Conciliarists at Constance had envisaged. And it was the position of the moderates that found expression in *Haec sancta.* Those moderates ascribed to the general council not only a "control function" over the pope in cases of dire emergency but also some more continuously operating restraint upon the abuse of papal power. Thus, while there may be some room for argument with Küng about the way in which he interprets the claims made in *Haec sancta* for the Conciliar authority, our own analysis would suggest that, if anything, he errs on the side of *underestimating* rather than exaggerating the range of those claims. Whether or not he also underestimates the practical consequences of his own conclusions for the life of the Church today remains now to be seen.

131

CHAPTER 5

An Uncommitted Theology?

(a) A Case of Deductive Timidity

> But I do not assert this, because it is dangerous to speak of
> this matter, possibly more dangerous than to speak of the
> Trinity or of the Incarnation of Jesus Christ our Saviour.
> (Jean Courtecuisse, *Tractatus de fide et ecclesia, romano
> pontifice et concilio generali.*[1])

These words occur in a treatise on papal and Conciliar prerogatives written by a French theologian in 1389, but they could be
taken, without too much injustice, to stand as the motto of those
contemporary Catholic writers who have addressed themselves
to that "neuralgic point" [2] in Catholic ecclesiological discourse—
the events of Constance and their implications for the relationship
between pope and universal Church today. This is certainly true
of Gill and of the authors of many of the encyclopedia articles at
which we glanced in the last chapter. It is only a little less true of
Jedin and Franzen. In view of his initial failure to draw the obvious conclusion from his own historical findings,[3] it is true to a

1. In Jean Gerson, *Opera Omnia,* ed. Louis Ellies Dupin (Antwerp,
1706), I, col. 882. Courtecuisse had just ventured the opinion that *if* the
pope is possessed of any power of coercive jurisdiction beyond the power
of excommunicating he has such a power from the emperor or the community of the faithful but not immediately from Christ.

2. The expression is that of K. A. Fink, "Zur Beurteilung des Grossen
Abendländischen Schismas," *Zeitschrift fur Kirchengeschichte,* LXXIII
(1962), 335.

3. See his "Le conciliarisme aux conciles de Constance et de Bâle," in
B. Botte *et al., Le Concile de Constance: Contribution à l'histoire de la
vie conciliare de l'église* (Chevetogne-Paris, 1960), pp. 180-181.

certain extent even of de Vooght. And it is also true of the editors of *Unam sanctam,* the series in which his book appeared.

For reasons best known to themselves, these editors saw fit to preface de Vooght's book with an *avertissement.* In it they note that if his study leads to an historical conclusion, it leads also to a theological problem. The conclusion being that *Haec sancta* received the approbation of Martin V and Eugenius IV and is a valid Conciliar enactment, the theological problem raised thereby needs no emphasizing. What does deserve emphasis, they seem to feel, is that de Vooght and Küng (whom they also mention) attach so much importance to the fact of papal approbation of the decree, for that should exonerate them from the charge of having condoned Conciliarism. What also deserves emphasis is the fact that Jedin, while not unsympathetic with the views of these two men, has tried to minimize their impact, and that they (the editors) agree with Jedin—except on one point of doctrine, and that point, they hasten to add, *can* be integrated with Vatican II's doctrine of collegiality. For the *Constitution on the Church,* which proclaims that doctrine, is at least "favorable" towards the thesis that the general council holds its authority immediately from Christ, "since the council is only the assembled college [of bishops] and the college is stated to have been instituted as such by Christ". But in certain circumstances (the examples given are the pope's insanity, his presumed death, his imprisonment without prospect of release), the council can assemble and act without him on the understanding that its decisions must later be confirmed or at least "freely accepted" by the pope. And "is that not what happened at Constance for everything that it had done 'conciliariter'?" Hence, while it would be improper to attribute to the council a superiority over the pope, it is within the bounds of orthodoxy to ascribe to it a certain "priority" (*antériorité*).[4]

---

4. Paul de Vooght, *Les pouvoirs du Concile et l'autorité du pape au Concile de Constance* (Paris, 1965), pp. 9-11. The passage of *Lumen Gentium* (ch. 3, § 22) on which this edifice rests reads as follows: "A council is

What is interesting here is not only the fact that the editors felt it necessary to attach this note to the book or the extreme caution with which they strove to make their point, but also their willingness in so doing to reshape boldly the history of Constance and to force the meaning of a dogmatic constitution only just promulgated by Vatican II.[5] What is interesting, too, is their implied justification of this extraordinary procedure by classifying de Vooght's book as one of those studies which "must be done in order to clarify the Constitution *Lumen gentium* in the light of history, *and history in the light of the doctrine which has been promulgated*".[6] For what is involved here, I would suggest, is the employment of a classic Catholic stratagem for avoiding the necessity of admitting radical discontinuities in the history of the Church (*semper idem*!), and it has to be remarked that it is no less deplorable or corrupting or destructive of the truth when used to promote the attainment of a progressive goal than when deployed as part of a conservative maneuver to perpetuate the *status quo*.

Editors, however, have often to cope with problems and pres-

---

never ecumenical unless it is confirmed or at least accepted as such by the successor of Peter. It is the prerogative of the Roman Pontiff to convoke these councils, to preside over them, and to confirm them. The same collegiate power can be exercised in union with the Pope by the bishops living in all parts of the world, provided that the head of the college calls them to collegiate action, or at least so approves or freely accepts the united action of the dispersed bishops, that it is made a true collegiate act." In Walter M. Abbott, ed., *The Documents of Vatican II* (London and New York, 1966), p. 44.

5. My own reading of the passage in question (see adove, p. 134, n. 4), of the related *Decree on the Bishops' Pastoral Office in the Church* (1965; Abbott, *Documents,* pp. 396-429), of Pope Paul's *motu proprio* establishing the Synod of Bishops, *Apostolica Sollicitudo* (1965; Abbott, Documents, pp. 720-724), and of the conciliar discussions on the *Constitution* in so far as they have been accessible to me, all lead me to the conclusion that the interpretation of the text which these editors give is a forced one, corresponding neither with the intentions of the council fathers nor with the seemingly obvious meaning of the passage cited (de Vooght, *Pouvoirs*, p. 10, n. 1), for that passage refers to subsequent papal acceptance as making "a true collegial act" of "the united action of the bishops" dispersed "in the various parts of the world"; i.e., *not* acting as a council.

6. De Vooght, *Pouvoirs*, p. 11 (italics mine).

sures that authors do not, and perhaps more revealing than the reaction of these particular editors to de Vooght's and Küng's finding in favor of the continuing validity of *Haec sancta* is Küng's own attitude to this same conclusion. This attitude is not constant but shifts, as might be expected, in accordance with the context in which the ecclesiology of Constance is discussed. Thus, one would look in vain for any extended treatment of these matters in Küng's latest and most distinguished work—a masterly ecclesiological treatise which has been described as "far and away the best Catholic text [on the Church] available".[7] Based resoulutely upon a close and painstaking analysis of the New Testament evidence, only about a fifth of the book is devoted, as a result, to the topic of ecclesiastical office and only a tenth to the question of the Petrine ministry. Given the methodology adopted and the conclusions it yields, one might be inclined to expect that the whole question of the ecclesiology of Constance would be bypassed in this context as simply redundant. That is not, however, the case.

Working outward from the principles that "there are no irreformable areas in the Church", doctrinal or institutional, and that "the only measure for renewal in the Church is the original Gospel of Jesus Christ himself; the only concrete guide . . . the apostolic Church" (p. 341), Küng goes on to draw a whole series of devastating conclusions. "A frightening gulf separates the Church of today from the original constitution of the Church" (p. 413). Indeed, as the New Testament reveals, that "original constitution" was itself pluriform. Even when the two basic church-types—Palestinian and Pauline—coalesced, with the latter obscuring the former, the differences from modern ecclesiological forms are still more striking than the similarities. Thus the idea of a separate priestly caste, "after pagan and Judaic patterns, standing between God and man," is contrary to the New Testa-

---

7. The book is *The Church,* trans. Ray and Rosaleen Ockenden (New York, 1968). The remark occurs in Michael Novak's review in *The New York Times Book Review,* May 6, 1968, 20.

ment message—which is the message "of the *one* mediator and high priest Jesus Christ and that of the priesthood of all believers" (p. 383). "Permanent public ministries" were certainly exercised in the New Testament communities; the basis of these, however, was not "law or power, knowledge or dignity, but *service*" (p. 392). Nor is it possible "to draw clear theological and dogmatic lines of division" between the three ministries —those pertaining to presbyters, *episkopoi* and deacons—that eventually became so prominent. These divisions do reflect time-honored canonical arrangements, but they "should not be mistaken for dogmatic necessities" (p. 429). Nor, again, should the apostolic succession of these pastoral ministries be seen as

something that occurs automatically or mechanically with the laying on of hands. Faith is a prerequisite and a condition; it must be active in the spirit of the apostles. This succession does not exclude the possibility of error or failure, and so must be tested by the faithful as a whole. [P. 442.]

And so on. Even if "most of what is said is here [in Küng's book] is common currency among working theologians",[8] the overall impact is nonetheless breathtaking. At least, it is breathtaking to anyone whose disposition is such that theoretical conclusions arrived at point insistently and disquietingly in the direction of practical consequences to be striven for. But, then, there is in this book a marked disparity between the boldness with which Küng draws his theoretical conclusions and the caution with which he assesses their implications and sidles up to the matter of practical consequences. His treatment of the papal office illustrates very clearly the nature of this disparity. When he comes to discuss papal infallibility he says nothing beyond the fact that it is "only a special aspect of the infallibility of the Church" (p. 449). Unexceptionable enough, were it not for

8. See Daniel J. O'Hanlon, S.J., "Restructuring the Theology of the Church," *National Catholic Reporter*, May 8, 1968, 11.

the fact that earlier in the book he has described this latter infallibility as "a fundamental remaining in the truth, which is not
disturbed by individual errors", and has noted that it is "not
directly demonstrable from the New Testament" that this infallibility "has as a necessary consequence the *a priori,* unquestionable and *verifiable* infallibility of particular *statements*" (p.
342). For it is, surely, precisely the infallibility of particular
papal statements that the definition of Vatican I endorses.

On the matter of the papal primacy, the New Testament, it
seems, is similarly inconclusive. Küng insists, however, that the
decisive thing "is not the historical aspect of a proven succession,
however valuable that may be. The decisive thing is succession
in the Spirit: in the Petrine mission and task, in the Petrine witness and ministry" (p. 463). This being so, a way back has to be
found from current papalist "primacy of dominion" to the original Petrine "primacy of service and ministry". But how is this to
be done? The task involved is a truly collossal one. Here, again,
there is an extraordinary disparity between the question asked
and the answer given. For Küng is willing to pin nearly all his
hopes on a voluntary renunciation by the popes of their spiritual
power, and, failing that, on a more widespread recognition in the
Church of the limitations with which the exercise of that spiritual
power is already circumscribed. And it is in *this* context that he
cites *Haec sancta* and the ecclesiology of Constance, referring
back to his discussion of these matters in his earlier book, *Structures of the Church* (pp. 452–3).

The atmosphere surrounding this line of argument is one of
unreality and strain.[9] The swing from what amounts to an almost agnostic appraisal of the whole question of a scripturally
validated papal primacy to a delicately diplomatic insistence on

9. It surely takes a certain amount of rather desperate wishful thinking
to be able to see in "the voluntary laying aside of the tiara, the emblem
of papal dominion, by Paul VI" and in his other (unspecified) measures
of reform, evidence that that pontiff, like his predecessor, is concerned to
effect "an evangelical renunciation of spiritual power", *The Church,* p. 472.

the continuing validity of the Constance decrees reflects a truly
enormous scaling down in the calibre of the theological weaponry
being deployed. And the discussion of the issue in *Structures of
the Church*, to which Küng refers us and which, presumably, he
still regards as adequate, accentuates that process still further. As
its title suggests, the focus of *Structures of the Church* is a much
narrower one than that of *The Church*—to which, we are told, it
is to be related as a prolegomenon. In it Küng sets himself the task
of sketching out a theology of general councils and of the
relationship of pope to councils. In so doing, one of his fundamental axioms is "that, in no case, should questions of dogma
be made out of existing laws and ceremonial".[10] "A *binding
theology* of ecumenical councils cannot be simply deduced from
the present regulations of the *Codex Juris Canonici*", even if
most of "the school manuals" have tried to do precisely that
(p. 229).

This is especially true of the fundamental provisions laid
down in canon 222 of the Code, namely, that "there cannot be an
ecumenical council which is not convoked by the Roman Pontiff"
and that "the Roman Pontiff presides over an ecumenical council
in person or through his delegates; he establishes and desig-
nates the matter to be handled and the order to be followed; he
transfers, suspends, and dissolves the council and confirms its decrees".[11] It is certain that these provisions accord with "present-
day Church discipline", but it is certain, too, that they do not
reflect the procedures followed at all of the councils which the
Church has come to recognize as ecumenical, and it is equally
certain that they cannot be regarded as grounded in divine law.
Hence one cannot exclude the possibility that in cases of emergency the convocation of a council could still originate from the
episcopate or even from the laity (p. 329). Indeed, one would

10. *Structures of the Church*, trans. Salvator Attanasio (New York,
1964), p. 17.
11. *Codex Juris Canonici* (1917), can. 222.

do well to be aware of the fact that the legal principle stipulating the necessity of papal convocation, direction and approbation stems ultimately from a ninth-century forgery, the Pseudo-Isidorian decretals (p. 323). So, too, the principle enshrined in canon 1556 in the formula: "The First see is under the judgment of nobody" [12]—although this time it is a sixth-century forgery that is the source, and modern canonists in taking the principle over from the *Decretum* of Gratian took care also to omit the qualifying phrase which was contained in that version and which submitted the pope to judgment in the event of his lapsing into heresy (p. 251).[13]

Clearly a promising context in which to examine the ecclesiology of Constance, and it is in this context that Küng is led to conclude in favor of the dogmatic validity of *Haec sancta*. But it should be noted that it is not really in this context that he goes on to analyze the significance of that conclusion. Across the line of his argument falls the long shadow cast by the definitions of Vatican I. As a result, he seems content to subordinate the ecclesiology of Constance to that of Vatican I, to understand *Haec sancta* in terms of the teaching of that council, or, more precisely, to understand it only in terms of the room left by that teaching and by the 1917 Code of Canon Law for the existence of limitations upon the exercise of the papal authority. These limitations are not very impressive, but they include, Küng tells us, the possibility that the pope by lapsing into insanity or heresy (the fomenting of schism being tantamount to heresy) forfeits *ipso facto* his papal authority.

Catholic tradition says that even a pope, if he becomes heretical or schismatic, loses his office and that in such a case he cannot appeal to the legal principle: "No one can judge the first see". The question that the CIC [1917 Code of Canon Law] does not answer is: Who

12. *Ibid.,* can. 1556.
13. See above, ch. 3, pp. 80 ff.

is to judge? The answer of Catholic tradition and in particular that of the ecumenical Council of Constance is entirely clear: The *Church* judges, the Church in her valid representation . . . an ecumenical council by human convocation. [P. 311.]

As the above quotation reveals, however, the judgment of the council in these cases is by no means "the cause of the pope's loss of office. It is simply a "declarative judgment," a "legally valid confirmation" of that loss of office making it "legally effective for the public of the Church". And in the light of Vatican I, of "present-day canonistic theory", and of *Haec sancta* (taken in that order of precedence), it is only in this sense that one can speak at all of a "superiority" of general council over pope (p. 287). In all of this, it should be noted, no reference is made to the Constance assertion that popes are subject to Conciliar authority on matters pertaining to Church reform.

Now quite clearly a great gulf separates this type of thinking from the thinking of the fathers of Constance when they promulgated *Haec sancta* and moved to depose the rival claimants to the papacy. And the extreme caution evident in Küng's formulations here is light years away from the boldness he shows in exposing the sharp contrast between the scriptural vision of the Petrine office and the "primacy of dominion" exercised by the popes today. No doubt it would be somewhat unfair to recall at this point Charles Davis's charge that "the present time . . . is characterized by an escape into theology", that we today are "dazzled by what is fundamentally an uncommitted theology, deluged with a spate of theoretical ideas that are not thought through consistently to their ecclesiastical, social and political consequences".[14] After all, Davis speaks also of the prevailing circumstances under which Catholic theologians must perforce move mounds of "ecclesiastical rubble" in order to win for

14. Charles Davis, *A Question of Conscience* (London and New York, 1967), pp. 190 and 236.

140

themselves even the narrowest of theological breathing spaces. Hans Küng has certainly had to move more "ecclesiastical rubble" for us than most, the problem of pope and council is, indeed, as he himself says, an extremely delicate one, and the cause of ecumenism—central to all of his theological endeavors—is not to be advanced by fomenting strife and disunity within one's own church.

(b) A Time for Candor

But no more will that cause of ecumenism be advanced by ignoring the strife and disunity that already exist, or by discreetly bypassing what has emerged today as the single most powerful cause of that strife and disunity. And what is that cause? Nothing other than Pope Paul's characteristically *curial* conception of the papal authority, his current mode of exercising it, the ambivalent attitude he has adopted towards the theological vision embodied in the major documents of Vatican II,[15] and the demoralizing backing and filling that this has caused among the ranks of the bishops—so many of whom, despite the conciliar experience and the evidence of their progressive council votes, seem, for instance, to have found it difficult to decide whether or not they were really supposed to take seriously the doctrine of collegiality. As a result, the "primacy of dominion" characteristic of the modern papacy, long an obstacle on the road to Christian unity, is now in process of becoming a stumbling block to Catholics themselves. "Almost singlehandedly, Pope Paul has tried to keep the lingering vestiges of Ultramontanism alive, and with it the transcendence of his own office. Most signs point

15. And *a fortiori* towards the broadening out of that vision to comprehend a theological landscape glimpsed only fitfully during the debates of Vatican I; although, in this case, his attitude is hostile and uncomprehending rather than ambivalent.

in one direction: he is failing." [16] And as the gap widens between the post-conciliar thinking of liberal and radical theologians alike and the nagging pre-conciliar exhortations emanating with distressing frequency from Rome (and echoed dutifully from a thousand diocesan chanceries), that "primacy of dominion" is serving increasingly to erode the credibility not only of the papal office itself but also of ecclesiastical authority in general.

This fact surely needs no underlining today, in the wake of the pope's disastrous decision to reaffirm in a highly authoritative fashion, demanding from the faithful "loyal and full assent" [17] the traditional ban on the use of all artificial methods of birth control. Because of the sensitive nature of the issue, the wide range of its effects and side-effects, and the vast shift that has taken place over the last few years in the thinking of so many Catholics, lay and clerical alike, this decision seems destined to be the most deeply divisive initiative taken at least by any twentieth-century pope. Given the conflict, clamor and confusion which currently prevails, it is hard to predict what the ultimate outcome is likely to be. But on the basis of the present state of affairs, the most plausible *scenario* one can envisage would have the pope, curia and bishops confronting the majority of the most distinguished Catholic theologians, with priests dithering between the two camps, and laity ignoring both.

And yet, in the light of contemporary ecclesiological discussion the alignment of the bishops with the pope on this doctrinal issue (if not necessarily on its pastoral implications) is a truly extraordinary development. For one of the clearest messages conveyed by the pope's encyclical (and a good deal clearer than the

16. Editorial in *Commonweal,* July 12, 1968, 451.
17. Thus Msgr. Ferdinardo Lambruschini, in announcing the encyclical, declared it to be "an authentic pronouncement of the church magisterium, binding the consciences of all Roman Catholics . . . without any possibility of ambiguity"; as reported in *The New York Times,* July 30, 1968, 1, col. 8.

arguments undergirding its moral teaching) is the blunt fact that Pope Paul VI, despite his formal approbation of Vatican II's *Dogmatic Constitution on the Church,* simply does not take seriously the teaching on collegiality embodied in that constitution. On this most pressing of pastoral problems the bishops were not consulted in any systematic fashion. Unlike *Time* magazine, it seems, they had to await the formal promulgation of the encyclical in order to discover the thinking of the "ordinary magisterium" of the Church—a bizarre state of affairs. Indeed, so far were some of them from anticipating the final outcome that the practice of leaving the decision on means of family limitation to the consciences of married couples themselves—already unstated policy in many dioceses—was raised to the level of official diocesan policy as recently as the spring of 1968 by the local ordinaries of Cuernavaca in Mexico and Munich and Trier in Germany.

As a result, the most distressing feature of the chorus of episcopal assent which swelled immediately after the encyclical was issued is surely the fact that that assent (sometimes anguished, occasionally gleeful, frequently sycophantic) [18] would seem to indicate the shameful willingness of perhaps the majority of the bishops themselves to acquiesce, publicly at least, in the pope's negation of collegiality—despite the fact that that teaching itself emanated from "the highest magisterial organ in the Church", the general council in which they themselves had participated.[19]

It might conceivably be possible to dismiss this appraisal as harsh and exaggerated if the encyclical *Humanae vitae* stood alone. But that is far from being the case. The warning signals

18. Some of the most strident voices have been American. See, e.g., the statements of Bishop Tracey of Baton Rouge, Bishop Hogan of Altoona-Johnstown, Pa., and Archbishop Alter of Cincinnati; cited in *National Catholic Reporter,* August 14, 1968, 8.

19. For its dogmatic status, see the *Addendum* to the *Constitution on the Church* in Abbott, *Documents,* pp. 97-98.

have been flying at Rome for several years now. During those years the Church has witnessed on this issue of collegiality a striking counterpoint between cautious affirmation in theory and unambiguous negation in practice. Thus the Vatican Council in proclaiming the doctrine of collegiality affirmed the co-responsibility of the bishops with the pope in the exercise of the jurisdictional and teaching power of the Church. At the same time the pope, having tried unsuccessfully to introduce into the text of the *Constitution on the Church* the phrase "the Roman pontiff is responsible to God alone", and having had appended to that constitution an explanatory note which clearly reflected the fear that collegiality might endanger the papal authority as traditionally conceived,[20] now withdrew from the bishops assembled in council and arrogated to himself alone the task of deciding what were already emerging as two of the most critical pastoral problems within the Church: the question of clerical celibacy and that of family limitation.

Similarly, the Bishops Synod of 1967. Touted both in advance and in retrospect as a practical manifestation of collegiality, it seems to have fallen short of that goal. Being, as presently constituted, a merely advisory assembly, with "its potential deliberative (decision-making) function" deriving not "from God through the episcopal consecration of its members, but from the pope", it does not really fulfill all the requirements of "a truly collegial act", as that is defined in the provisions of the *Constitution on the Church*.[21] It was the pope who chose the topics for discussion and who determined the agenda. Despite pressure to

20. The note is in Abbott, *Documents,* pp. 98-101.
21. This is the view expressed at Rome in 1967 by Guiseppe Alberigo of the University of Bologna; see Francis X. Murphy and Gary MacEoin, *Synod '67: A New Sound in Rome* (Milwaukee, 1968), pp. 18-19; cf. *Apostolica Sollicitudo,* Pope Paul's *motu proprio* of September 15, 1965, establishing the Synod of Bishops (in Abbott, *Documents,* pp. 720-724). Section II of that document reads as follows: "By its very nature it is the task of the Synod of Bishops to inform and give advice. It may also have

get them included, the question of clerical celibacy and that of family limitation—no less pressing now than they had been during the council—were again excluded from synodal consideration, even despite the fact that the bishops had, this time, no decision-making powers.

Not that the Synod in its actual debates was any less free or any more pliant than the council had been. It rebuffed in no uncertain terms a doctrinal initiative of the indefatigable curial *immobilisti,* which took the form this time of a position paper presented to the Synod by the Congregation for the Faith under the leadership of Cardinal Ottaviani. Had the Synod approved this position paper, then "this document as drawn up by the ex-Holy Office," it has been said, "would have served as the starting point for the preparation of a papal statement, almost certainly an encyclical, which would have recalled all too well Pius IX's encyclical, *Quanta Cura,* and its annex, the 'Syllabus of Eighty Erroneous Propositions'." [22]

In the event, however, the Synod rejected the document, and, in its final report, approved the submission of two proposals to the pope. The first of these envisaged the establishment of a commission composed of theologians "of diverse schools", men "who reside in various parts of the Western and Eastern Church", who are to be selected by the pope on the basis of recommendations made by the episcopal conferences, and whose duty it will be, acting with all lawful academic freedom, to assist the Holy See and especially the Sacred Congregation for the Doctrine of the Faith". The second proposal suggested that "having heard the views of the Episcopal Conference, the Holy See draw up a positive pastoral declaration concerning questions involved in

deliberative power, *when such power is conferred on it by the Sovereign Pontiff,* who will in such cases confirm the decisions of the Synod" (italics mine). Cf. *Constitution in the Church,* ch. 3, § 22; *ibid.,* pp. 42-44.

22. *Informations Catholiques Internationales,* as cited in Murphy and MacEoin, *Synod '67,* p. 88.

the doctrinal crisis of today, so that the faith of the people of God may be given secure direction." [23]

All this, no doubt, very promising and hopeful, the more so in that it represents the views of the majority of those speaking on behalf of the residential bishops, the men most directly involved in pastoral work. The promise, however, has not yet been realized and the hope has now been dissipated. No such "positive pastoral declaration" has been made, and, to my knowledge, the proposed theological commission, so very badly needed at Rome, has not been established. Instead, on June 30, 1968, Pope Paul took it upon himself to issue his own "new Credo". In addition to reiterating the formulas of the Nicene Creed and speaking, despite Vatican II's *Decree on Ecumenism,* of the Roman Catholic Church as the "one only Church", this "Credo" went on to reaffirm the doctrines of the Immaculate Conception, the Assumption, papal infallibility and original sin (as defined by the Council of Trent), while referring to the real presence as "very appropriately called by the Church transubstantiation". The whole statement, with its warnings about the contemporary "passion for change and novelty" and its references to the "disturbance and perplexity in many faithful souls", is, to say the least, preconciliar in tone and content—more so, indeed, than the curial position paper and profession of faith which the Synod of Bishops had rejected only nine months previously as entirely unsuitable.[24] It witnesses very dramatically, then, to the wide gap that has opened up, not only between the pope's thinking and that of the "establishment" theologians of the day, but also (and even more disturbingly) between his thinking and that of a broad majority of the episcopate.

What emerges, then, is a fairly consistent pattern. At the heart of that pattern may well lie a certain incoherence in the con-

23. Text in Murphy and MacEoin, *Synod '67,* Appendix 6, pp. 221-222.
24. For that profession of faith, see Murphy and MacEoin, *Synod '67,* Appendix 5, pp. 213-214.

ciliar formulation of the doctrine of collegiality itself. Of that formulation Charles Davis has said that "there are grounds for thinking that little more has been done than with verbal dexterity to juxtapose two incompatible views of Church government", [25] and it is true, certainly, that those grounds become very strong if the explanatory note which the pope had attached to the text is indeed to be taken as "an authentic norm of interpretation".[26] But even if that is not the case, even if the formulation is a coherent one, papal policy has itself constituted a *de facto* negation of the doctrine.

The recent papal decision on birth control, and the manner in which that decision was reached, form merely the most striking strand in the pattern. The pope has since spoken of the anguish he felt and the suffering he endured in his struggle to arrive at a decision. "Never as at this point," he has said, "have we felt the burden of our office." "How often, humanly speaking, we have felt the inadequacy of our humble person for the formidable apostolic obligation of having to pronounce on the matter." [27] Such sentiments may do him credit as a man, but they serve also to make the course of action he chose to follow even harder to comprehend. It was *his* decision, after all, to keep the issue out of the council, and, later on, out of the episcopal Synod. It was also his decision to reject the majority finding of the representative commission he had appointed. It was his decision, again, it seems, to ignore even the worries expressed by some of the minority of that commission concerning the adequacy of the traditional and discredited natural-law argument. His isolation in the handling of the issue was, therefore, of his own choosing,

25. *A Question of Consicence,* p. 122. Davis adds: "Evidence is still awaited that episcopal collegiality can be made effective without modifying the content and implications of the definition of papal primacy in a manner so far bitterly resisted. The set-up of the Synod of Bishops does more to ensure papal primacy than to make episcopal collaboration genuinely effective."

26. See Abbott, *Documents,* p. 98, n. 3.

27. See *National Catholic Reporter,* August 7, 1968, 1-2.

and that choice is explicable neither on pastoral nor on doctrinal grounds. His earlier letter reaffirming in absolute terms the discipline of priestly celibacy failed to halt the spread of debilitating and demoralizing disagreement on that matter, and that should surely have served as a warning. It should have indicated to him that on an issue of the magnitude of birth control, and with its world-wide impact, it would be the better part of pastoral wisdom for a directive claiming and aspiring to bind the consciences of the faithful to emanate, if it was not to divide the Church still further, from as broadly representative an organ of the magisterium as possible. And if it is hard to imagine on what prudential pastoral grounds the pope should have prevented the council from grappling with the issue, it is equally difficult to discern any doctrinal reason for that extraordinary course of action. After all, Vatican II itself taught that the unity of the faith is preserved in the Church because the same Holy Spirit guides pope, college of bishops, and faithful alike.[28] The pope can hardly have thought that the college of bishops, like the majority of the commission, was likely to endorse an erroneous position which he himself would then have had to reject. Or could he?

After Pope Paul had issued his "new Credo", Dr. Ramsey, Archbishop of Canterbury, remarked that "since the Vatican Council began to distinguish between the more fundamental dogmas and the less fundamental ones, I was surprised that particular Roman Catholic Dogmas, like the immaculate conception and papal infallibility were inserted along with the tenets of the Nicene Creed." [29] But perhaps he should not have been so sur-

28. *Constitution on the Church*, ch. 3, § 25; Abbott, *Documents*, p. 49. This passage refers explicitly to the infallible teaching of pope and/or episcopal college. But in the light of the extravagant claims currently being made for what seems to be a rather one-sided activity of the Holy Spirit in the current doctrinal division it is surely not irrelevant.

29. Quoted in a dispatch from Uppsala in *The New York Times*, Wednesday, July 10, 1968, 10; cf. the *Decree on Ecumenism*, § 11, where it is stated that "the manner and order in which Catholic belief is expressed should in no way become an obstacle to dialogue with our brethren", and

prised. Those doctrines, along with that of the Assumption which was also inserted, are intimately associated, after all, with the supreme magisterial claims of the modern papacy. So, too, though to a somewhat lesser degree, is the teaching on birth control affirmed once more in the recent encyclical. And this, surely is the key to an understanding of current papal policy. Some clerics (including Msgr. Austin Vaughan, current president of the American Catholic Theological Society,) have admitted that their own objections to a change in the traditional teaching on family limitation were grounded not so much on an apprehension of the immorality of contraception itself as on the fact that the Church had affirmed that traditional teaching so forcefully in the past. "If there had been a change," Msgr. Vaughan has said, "it would have been extremely difficult to point to any area of the ordinary magisterium that might not change in the future." [30] Undoubtedly an astounding admission, for it reveals a cast of mind in which the need to preserve the authority of the institution takes precedence over the commitment to serve the people of God and the duty to discover and proclaim the truth. But given Pope Paul's admission of the obligation he felt to the teaching of his papal predecessors, and given his frequently attested concern to preserve "the transcendence of his own office", this would seem also, alas, to be his own cast of mind. All very human, of course, but no less scandalizing because of that. Indeed, given the persistent attempts to claim for the congregations of the Roman *curia* a monopoly on guidance by the Holy Spirit, it is, perhaps, even a little too human.

What we are witnessing today, therefore, is a situation in which the preservation of the papal authority, as conceived and exercised in the century since Vatican I, is being given precedence

where Catholic theologians are exhorted "when comparing doctrines" to "remember, that in Catholic teaching there exists an order or 'hierarchy' of truths, since they vary in their relationship to the foundation of the Christian faith". In Abbott, *Documents,* p. 354.

30. As reported in the *National Catholic Reporter,* August 7, 1968, 4, 9.

in papal policy over the well-being of the universal Church (or, less unfairly, is being identified with it in curial policy and in the mind of the pope). It is a situation in which the waves of reform liberated by the Second Vatican Council are breaking in vain upon the rock of Peter, a situation in which an already existing crisis of faith is being exacerbated rather than diminished by papal initiative, a situation in which the pope is increasingly in danger of separating himself from the body of the Church. At such a critical juncture in the life of the Church, the turbulent history of the Great Schism becomes suddenly less remote, the ecclesiology of Constance takes on an unexpected relevance, and the discovery of the dogmatic validity of the decree *Haec sancta* becomes a matter of immediate and pressing public concern.

It is no time, then, for timidity, or for discretion, or for "prudence" (that most disabling of all Catholic virtues!). It is a time, rather, for candor; indeed, however clichéd the expression, a time for confrontation, and confrontation at the very outset of the theoretical implications and practical consequences which must flow from the long overdue recognition of the status of *Haec sancta*. The conclusions set forth in the next chapter represent my own attempt, therefore, at such a confrontation. I proffer them because I believe them to be true; but, in an age in which every man is forced willy-nilly to be his own theologian, I am far from believing that they will eliminate the likelihood of argument or dissent. On one point, however, I am quite certain: that it is long since time for the argument on this issue to begin.

CHAPTER 6

Towards a Provisional Ecclesiology

(a) A Message to Conservatives

In the last few years it has become something of a commonplace to discern within the ranks of the opinion-making minority of Catholics three broad (and partially overlapping) groups: (i) the conservatives, whose sympathy with the pastoral and doctrinal *aggiornamento* attempted by Vatican II is minimal and who see it as their mission to defend existing ecclesiastical structures and procedures; (ii) the liberals or progressives, who, in a majority at the time of Vatican II, welcomed with excitement and relief the new departures taken at that council, and who see the task of the Church today to be one of doctrinal development and structural change along the lines indicated at that time; (iii) the radicals, hardly heard from when the council first met, but today a growing group which is increasingly separating itself from the second and is concerned decreasingly with the matter of structural or institutional change—or even with the very existence of the church-institution itself. The members of this group seek to fulfil their Christian commitment by active engagement in the great social causes of the day and by participation in loosely organized, *ad hoc*, "post-ecumenical" religious groupings. Their attitude towards the church-institution is rarely one of outright rejection, but aspires, at least, to be one, rather, of creative disaffiliation.

The discovery of the dogmatic validity of *Haec sancta* and the concomitant rehabilitation of the ecclesiology of Constance has something, I believe, to say to all three of these groups. It has a message for conservatives; it offers a chance to liberals; it extends

151

a hope to radicals. Doubtless it speaks most directly to liberals, today the most harried of these three groups. But it would be a pity if radicals dismissed it as a redundancy, and, given the current crisis of papal authority, the fact that it proffers a message to conservatives at all could well be the most important thing about it.

What, then, is that message? It may be summed up under two headings: the autonomy of history and the limitation of papal authority.

(i) *The autonomy of history:* If the general argument elaborated in the preceding chapters has proved anything, it has surely proved that without sacrificing one's intellectual integrity one cannot subordinate the past to the pressing demands of present-day theological convictions or canonistic regulations. To say this, of course, is simply to say something cognate to what modern scripture scholars have themselves had to say about the traditional textbook manipulation of the Scriptures, with its shuffling of proof-texts and its alignment of scriptural passages (often in incongruous juxtaposition) behind the theological option being defended.

But, then, conservatives are often curiously unmoved by arguments grounded in scripture—at least, in scripture as understood in the light of modern bible scholarship. A Küng can insist in vain that one must not take the *status quo* of the modern Church as any "absolute norm", that one "must measure it against the original message of Christ which it claims as its foundation", that "one can only know what the Church should be if one also knows what it was originally".[1] To this, the conservative is prone to reply: "On the contrary, only by knowing what the Church is now can one really know what it must have been originally." For what, after all, *is* the "original message of Christ"? How has

1. Hans Küng, *The Church,* trans. Ray and Rosaleen Ockenden (New York, 1968), pp. 292 and ix.

it been mediated to us? In what way are we to understand it? Is it not the Church that selected from among the numerous books claiming divine inspiration those which were to be accorded the status of revelation and included within the canon of the Scriptures? And is it not the Church that expounds in an authoritative fashion the teaching that is to be found in those books? Nor in order to say this is it necessary to argue in Counter-Reformation terms from the alleged preservation by the Church of revealed truths that are not contained in the Scriptures but have been handed down by unbroken oral tradition. Instead, it may be sufficient to take one's stand on the more fashionable notion of the "coinherence of Scripture and Tradition" and the refusal to understand either in isolation from the faith that is preached and living in the Church today—always supposing, of course, that the ecclesiastical magisterium is the *sole* authentic interpreter of the way in which the life of the Church is to be understood.

Precisely because it is not open to being outflanked by such a maneuver, the argument from post-apostolic history may well be a less vulnerable mode of communicating unwelcome news to latter-day conservatives than is the argument from scripture— and herein lies the importance of our own historical arguments. We are dealing now, after all, not with *kerygma* but with history, and it is history mediated to us and accessible to us, not merely in the life and teaching of the Church but via a multitude of sources that escape the control of the Church and often resist its moulding influence. No historian, I assume, would today want to deny that the answers one gets from the historical data depend very much upon the questions one chooses to ask of those data. But no historian, likewise, would be willing to admit that it is permissible to substitute theological or canonistic criteria of interpretation for the historical when the answers one gets from one's chosen questions fail unhappily to coincide with the answers which modern dogmatic or canonistic formulations have already imposed.

Things really happened in the past. We can employ all sorts of stratagems in order to elude a realization of this fact, but we are likely to pay a heavy price for so doing. When we rush to bolt the door on the past we are likely to succeed only in turning the present into a prison. And it is we ourselves who are then the prisoners. Mere generalities, no doubt, but given the psychological make-up of the conservative—with his characteristic demand for clear static certainties preserved intact from the vicissitudes of time—those generalities may well be equally as important as the specifics to which we can now turn.

(ii) *The limitation of papal authority:* The decree *Haec sancta* possesses dogmatic validity. Those who, by a dogmatic manipulation of the historical data, wish to evade an admission of this fact should realize that by so doing they will succeed only in damaging their own cause, in undermining the already sagging credibility of the ecclesiastical authority they are so determined to defend. Nor will they do much better if, capitulating on the question of validity, they retreat to the imposing bulwarks of Vatican I and the Code of Canon Law, and, in assessing the implications of the decree and the practical consequences attendant upon its validity, determine to admit only such attenuated propositions as can find their way through those formidable defences.

Even if some of its crucial canons were not grounded in what have turned out to be medieval forgeries, let it be repeated that no binding theology concerning councils and the relation of popes to councils could be grounded in the current disciplinary arrangements enshrined in the 1917 Code. And whatever we are to make of Vatican I (and that problem we will confront in due course),[2] it has to be admitted that the papal authority, despite the autonomy of its day-to-day exercise, is in the last analysis subordinated to the authority which the whole Church can exercise via the agency of a general council at those times when difficulties

2. See below, this chapter, section (c), pp. 162 ff.

154

arise which concern the faith of the Church, are destructive of its unity, or relate to its reform. It has to be admitted, too, that this conciliar authority has in the past been exercised to the extent of deposing a pope who refused obedience to it in these matters, that it can, therefore, be so exercised again, and that what is involved in such an exercise is not simply the promulgation of a "declarative judgment" indicating that a pope by his heresy has ceased *ipso facto* to be pope, but a case of outright deposition, the exercise of a superior jurisdictional authority by virtue of which the man is separated from the office. What man by election has joined together, man by deposition, seems, can put asunder.

This last point deserves emphasis. Outright deposition or "declarative judgment", the end result may well be the same—the public recognition that a certain man has ceased to be pope—but the assumptions involved are very different indeed, and it should be realized that those medieval and modern canonists and theologians who insisted that the authority of a council could not reach beyond the rendering of a declaratory judgment, did so because they were intent on preserving the absolute nature of the maxim that the pope was subject to the judgment of no human authority. But that maxim we now know to have stemmed from a forgery. We know, equally, that medieval canon law (unlike modern) qualified it in the case of papal heresy, and that many medieval canonists, as a result, regarded the general council as possessed of the necessary authority to stand in judgment on the pope and to depose him if need be. We know, too, that the Conciliarists of Constance echoed that belief and acted in terms of it. And we should not overlook the fact that even after the papal restoration and the demise of the Conciliar movement, theologians of the stature of Cajetan, Cano, Soto and Suarez endorsed a very similar point of view.[3]

3. See Hans Küng, *Structures of the Church,* trans. Salvatore Attanasio (New York, 1964), pp. 308 ff. In Cajetan's case, the refusal to adopt the

Much of this, no doubt, "offensive to pious ears",[4] but only because the modern centuries, and especially the last one, have seen the rich and polyphonic variety of the Catholic ecclesiological tradition narrowed down increasingly to a single and insistently papalist melodic line. In terms of the tradition as a whole it would be much more offensive if the universal Church possessed no institutional means of defending itself against the depradations of a pope who had turned his back on the Gospel. And yet that is precisely what the significant silence of the 1917 Code on the problem of conflict situations between pope and church might lead one to believe. If the standard modern manuals on canon law teach otherwise, their insistence on the fact that insane popes or heretical popes or popes guilty of fomenting schism in the Church lose *ipso facto* their authority derives only from the canonistic and theological tradition that is most favorable to the high-papalist claim to immunity from judgment.[5] They ignore that other tradition which informed the thinking of the Conciliar theorists at Constance and which was given expression in the promulgation of *Haec sancta* and the deposition of the rival pontiffs. And, let it be said once more that if the legitimacy of these measures is denied, so, too, must be impugned, on any traditional interpretation of the notion of apostolic succession,[6] the legitimacy of all subsequent popes right down to the present.

But what does all this mean in practical terms today? It means at the very least, I would suggest, a de-canonization of the relevant sections of the 1917 Code. It means that bishops today

---

view that an heretical pope ceased *ipso facto* to be pope caused him some embarrassment in his polemics against Conciliar theory; see my "Almain and Major: Conciliar theory on the Eve of the Reformation," *American Historical Review*, LXX (1965), 673 ff.

4. See the comments of Kevin Smythe on Küng's *Structures*, "Forms of Church Government—A New Essay Examined," *Irish Theological Quarterly*, XXX (1963), 61-62.

5. See, e.g., F. X. Wernz and P. Videl, *Jus Canonicum* (Rome, 1943), II, pp. 513-521 and esp. p. 517.

6. And conservatives are presumably unlikely to embrace any re-interpretation such as that given by Küng; see *The Church*, pp. 354 ff.

should not feel, or be made to feel, for instance, that they have to accept with docility the curial insistence on total "papal" (that is, curial) control of agenda, modes of procedure and appointment of presiding officers in general councils, or, more pertinently, in the Synod of Bishops. Indeed, because the unilateral papal decision to withdraw from conciliar and synodal discussion two of the most pressing pastoral problems of the day has done so much to exacerbate the present crisis in the Church, they have very good reason to demand, in the interest of the general welfare, the limitation or abolition of that control.

Nor, as seems to be the case in the current furor over the birth control ruling, should they feel bound (or be made to feel bound) to align themselves with a papal teaching that has been arrived at via procedures tantamount to a negation of the conciliar teaching on collegiality. Nor should they, or anyone else, feel free to suggest, as Bishop Tracy of Baton Rouge has recently suggested, that there is no other authority in the world "under Catholic teaching, which can overrule an official pronouncement of the Pope",[7] or to demand of those Catholics who cannot in conscience accept such a pronouncement that they should either abandon their personal integrity or "leave the Church". Least of all, at the present moment, should they close their eyes to the fact that it may conceivably in the future become their painful duty to call upon a pope to resign his high office for the well-being of all the faithful.

All this, moderate enough and certainly relevant to the present situation, but doomed, I suspect, unless a further consequence is faced, to remain as much a matter of Utopian theory as those "concrete limits" on papal authority which, Küng points out, even the definitions of Vatican I left standing.[8] Only the liberal or progressive group can really be expected, and then with no degree of certainty, to face this further consequence. But if that group will indeed do so, it can expect to recover the initiative it

7. See the dispatch in the *National Catholic Reporter,* August 14, 1968, 8.
8. *Structures of the Church,* pp. 234 ff.; *The Church,* pp. 449 ff.

has lost in the postconciliar era to the reactionaries of the *curia,* on the one hand, and the revolutionaries of the "underground church" on the other.

(b) A Chance for Liberals

The difficulty involved here might well be described as hinging on the old distinction between the *quaestio juris* and the *quaestio facti.* The history of the late-fifteenth and early-sixteenth centuries tells us about many a churchman who was persuaded of the rectitude of Conciliar theory, with its corollary that in case of emergency a general council could assmble even without papal convocation, but who could never be convinced that such an emergency actually existed. On the *quaestio juris* they were with the Conciliarists; but not on the *quaestio facti.* The possibility of such a disjunction between admission in principle and denial in practice is even more likely to occur in the Church today. It is conceivable that conservatives might be able to bring themselves to admit the dogmatic validity of *Haec sancta* and to accept the fact that the ecclesiology of Constance cannot simply be dismissed as heterodox. It is conceivable, too, that they might also be willing to face up to the type of practical consequence of that admission discussed at the end of the last section. It is almost utterly inconceivable, however, that they should ever find it possible to admit that any dispute between pope and Church, however grave, could be grave enough to justify the assembly of a general council without explicit papal convocation, or contrary to the wishes of the pope.

Similarly, whatever their theoretical positions, even today it is difficult to imagine more than a handful of liberals being willing to take so harsh, so drastic, so divisive a step. And yet the dismal likelihood of their being faced in the future with the compelling need to take precisely such a step increases daily and their own disarray can only help accelerate the whole process. Despite the warning of Pope Paul's "new Credo" and the shattering blow of *Humanae vitae,* they remain wedded, it would seem, to the familiar delusions of gradualism. But, in the meantime, reform is in danger of being trivialized, the credibility of the whole institution crumbles, and the crisis of faith deepens. At the same time, deceived by the "prudence" of the bishops, sustained by the selective plaudits of *Osservatore Romano,* and stimulated, perhaps, by nostalgic curialist talk about a more vigorous exercise of papal authority in the future, the pope seems intent on separating himself in lonely schism from the thinking of most of the faithful.

Time is running out. It is running out on precisely the type of progressive reformism so dear to liberal hearts. Clearly what is needed is a new program of action, and it is needed *now.* And here the rediscovery of the validity of *Haec sancta* offers the liberals a chance (and perhaps their last chance) to seize the initiative again. For it means that no longer need anyone feel that to call upon the pope to summon a general council is to teeter precariously on the rim of heterodoxy. "Conciliarist" is no longer a word to be deployed exclusively by the resourceful purveyors of theological abuse. A general council is the only authority now capable of dealing with the critical situation that has developed in the Church.[9] It is imperative that the pope convoke a new council and that he should do so as swiftly as possible. But that convocation is likely to be forthcoming only if the dwindling group still dedicated to institutional reform is willing boldly to initiate the demand for such a council and to bring heavy and unrelenting pressure to bear, via the multitudinous lay and clerical associations already in existence, on pope and bishops alike. National bishops' conferences could hardly remain indif-

9. Since I wrote these words, the call for the assembly of a new council has been issued by the *National Catholic Reporter* (August 21, 1968), and, it seems, by others.

ferent to a massive public campaign in their churches on behalf of such a council, and it is hard to envisage the pope's being so foolhardy as to spurn such a demand if it won the support of a significant number of those conferences.[10]

Moreover, the real needs of the Church at the moment should take precedence over the dispositions of the 1917 Code. Pressure should be brought to bear, then, not simply on behalf of a new general council, but of a council much more broadly representative of the Church as a whole and much more fully in control of its own agenda, organization and modes of procedure than any of the great modern councils. On these matters, the message taught by facts of conciliar history is inescapable: on no dogmatic grounds can it be claimed that representation or voting rights have to be denied either to the theological and canonistic experts or to the lower clergy or to laymen or to laywomen.[11] If, as is often said, Vatican I was the council of the pope and Vatican II the council of the bishops, then it would be more than appropriate if the new council (shall we call it Vatican III?) turned out to be the council of the priests and laity.

If such a general council, so composed and so functioning, were to meet today, I have little doubt that it would vote to abolish, or at least to loosen, the bond which for centuries has made the conferring of full sacerdotal orders contingent upon a lifelong commitment to the celibate state. Still less do I doubt that it would hesitate to repudiate the excessive claims now being made for the authority and binding force of *Humanae vitae*. Use might possibly be made of some facesaving formula such as that recently adopted by the Dutch bishops.[12] But the conciliar teaching would almost certainly involve some indication that the

10. Cf. editorial in *National Catholic Reporter*, August 21, 1968.

11. Cf. Küng, *Structures*, pp. 74 ff.

12. See *National Catholic Reporter*, August 21, 1968. Given the teaching of Vatican II in the *Church in the Modern World*, it is hard to imagine that Vatican III could endorse *Humanae vitae*—See the remarks of Bernard Häring, "The Encyclical Crisis," *Commonweal*, September 6, 1968, 593-594.

position outlined in that encyclical is the position of the pope and not necessarily that of the whole Church, and it might well go so far as to indicate, at least implicitly, a rejection of that position.

More important in the long haul, however, than any specific steps it might take would be the very assembly of such a restructured council and under such extraordinary circumstances. In a recent and extremely pessimistic appraisal of the prospects for institutional reform in the Church, Rosemary Ruether has said that "there seems precious few handles for a constitutional reform of the ecclesiastical structure, since the only persons empowered to make such changes have both theoretical and vested interests in the old regime. How do you create a revolution in an autocratic regime which has no constitutional or ideological means of democratization?" [13] To this it may now be replied that the rehabilitation of the Conciliarist ecclesiology has furnished the ideological means and the assembly of Vatican III would provide the constitutional. For the fathers of such a council would hardly be tempted to limit themselves to treating the symptoms of the malaise afflicting the Church, and omit to attack the disease itself, which is in part institutional. They would be derelict in their duty if they failed to clarify the whole problem of authority in the Church, to initiate far-reaching reforms (perhaps along the lines of the Episcopal ecclesiastical structures) designed to balance the hierarchical elements with more representative and democratic structures, to separate legislative, administrative and judicial functions, to eliminate the secret and arbitrary procedures to which so many of the higher clergy still cling. And so on. It is unnecessary to elaborate on this point here. Tentative blueprints for such institutional reforms are to be found in the mental files of most liberal Catholics, and, of recent years, programs of this type have been analyzed in some detail by

13. In her article, "Schism of Consciousness," *Commonweal,* May 31, 1968, 328.

theologians and canonists alike.[14] What has been lacking has been simply the means to translate them into actuality.

(c) A Hope for Radicals

Heady stuff, no doubt, but the whole line of argument in the two previous sections leaves one very grave problem outstanding. Liberals may conceivably be content to operate within this frame of reference, but they can hardly deny that it is predicated on the twin assumptions that it is possible simply to sidestep the decrees of Vatican I and that it is legitimate to do so. And yet it is on these assumptions that the objections of both radicals and conservatives are likely to converge. Radicals, increasingly disenchanted with the whole business of structural reform and institutional change (and not without reason), will question the possibility or viability of such a procedure; conservatives, wedded to a belief in the infallibility of solemn conciliar definitions on particular points of doctrine, will question its legitimacy. And correctly so. Liberal theologians and ecumenists may share Küng's hope that given "an evangelical renunciation of spiritual power" by the successors of John XXIII "the offensive aspects of the definitions of Vatican I might become as immaterial as, for example, the *dictatus papae* (which is not even to be found in Denzinger's *Enchiridion*!)".[15] But even if such a development

14. For any such structural reform the replacement of the 1917 *Code of Canon Law* by something much less responsive to the *political* problematic is clearly a prerequisite. For the discussion surrounding the current proposed reform of the canon law; already under way but in the hands, alas!, of a Roman curial commission; see, e.g., Francis X. Murphy and Gary MacEoin, *Synod '67: A New Sound in Rome* (Milwaukee, 1968), pp. 52-72; Gregory Baum, *The Credibility of the Church Today: A Reply to Charles Davis* (London and New York, 1968), pp. 193 ff.; Petrus Huizing, "The Reform of the Canon Law," *Concilium* (Glen Rock, New Jersey, 1961), VIII, pp. 95-128.

15. *The Church*, p. 472.

were desirable, recent events have underlined its inherent improbability. The definitions of Vatican I have, therefore, to be confronted and a decision has to be arrived at concerning the relationship between them and *Haec sancta*.

The definitions in question are contained in the third and fourth chapters of the dogmatic constitution *Pastor aeternus*, defining, respectively, the primacy and infallibility of the Roman pontiffs. If we recall to mind the provisions of *Haec sancta* [16] for which we have claimed dogmatic validity, and if we cite the central passages of the definitions of primacy and infallibility, then the grave difficulties involved in the enterprise of reconciling these conciliar decrees will be immediately evident.

(i) The most important passages of the definition of primacy read as follows:

Accordingly we teach and declare that the Roman Church, by the disposition of the Lord, possesses the preeminence of ordinary power over all other churches, and that this power of jurisdiction of the Roman Pontiff, which is truly episcopal, is immediate. With respect to [this jurisdictional power], pastors and faithful of whatever rite and dignity are bound, both individually and collectively, by a duty of hierarchical subjection and of true obedience, not only in matters that pertain to faith and morals, but also in things pertaining to the discipline and government of the Church throughout the whole world; in such a way that, preserved in the unity with the Roman Pontiff both of communion and profession of the same faith, the Church of Christ may be one flock under one supreme pastor. This is the doctrine of Catholic truth, from which no one can deviate without losing his faith and salvation. . . . And since by the divine right of the Apostolic Primacy the Roman Pontiff is supreme in the universal Church, we teach also and declare that he is supreme judge of the faithful, resort to whose judgment can be had in all cases open to ecclesiastical decision. Indeed, the judgment of the Apostolic See, to which there is no higher authority, is not to be withdrawn by anyone, nor is it lawful for anyone to stand in judgment on its verdict.

16. For the text, see above, ch. 2, p. 75.

Wherefore, they stray from the right path of truth who affirm that it is lawful to appeal from the judgment of the Roman Pontiffs to an ecumenical council as if to an authority superior to the Roman Pontiff.

The canon attached to it goes as follows:

Therefore, if anyone says that the Roman Pontiff has only the duty of inspection or direction, but not the full and supreme power of jurisdiction in the universal Church, not only in matters that pertain to faith and morals, but also in those pertaining to the discipline and government of the Church throughout the whole world; or if [anyone says] that he has the more important part and not the complete fullness of this supreme power; or that this power of his is not ordinary and immediate in each and every church or over each and every pastor and member of the faithful; let him be anathema.[17]

(ii) And the definition of infallibility:

We, therefore, adhering faithfully to the tradition known from the beginning of the Christian faith . . . teach and define as a dogma divinely revealed: That the Roman Pontiff, when he speaks *ex cathedra* —that is, when fulfilling the office of pastor and teacher of all Christians, he defines a doctrine concerning faith or morals to be held by the universal Church—through the divine assistance promised to him in blessed Peter, enjoys that infallibility with which the divine Redeemer willed his Church to be endowed when defining doctrine concerning faith or morals; and, therefore, that such definitions of the Roman Pontiff are irreformable of themselves and not by virtue of the consent of the Church [*ex sese, non autem ex consensu Ecclesiae, irreformabiles esse*].

The canon attached:

If anyone, however, shall presume to contradict this our definition— which God forbid!—let him be anathema.[18]

17. H. Denzinger and A. Schönmetzer, *Enchiridion Symbolorum* (Rome, 1965), §§ 3060, 3063 and 3064; pp. 598-599.
18. Denzinger and Schönmetzer, §§ 3073 and 3074; pp. 601.

The prospect of attempting to bring these decrees into contact with *Haec sancta* is, at first glance, a truly daunting one. Four main contradictions seem to stand out immediately:

(i) Constance subordinates the pope to the general council (acting without the pope) in the three cases it mentions, and demands his obedience to the council on pain of punishment. Vatican I claims, in effect, that the pope is subject jurisdictionally and juridically to no external human authority. In virtue of this general and sweeping claim, subject, it seems, to no exception, it demands the "true obedience" of all the faithful both "individually and collectively".

(ii) Constance claims for the council in the three cases mentioned a superior authority to that of the pope. Vatican I denies that there is any authority superior to that of the pope.

(iii) The assertion that the council can ever possess an authority superior to that of the pope necessitates the admission that it may be legitimate, under certain circumstances, to appeal from pope to council. Indeed, the very action of the fathers at Constance in promulgating *Haec sancta* itself constitutes, in effect, such an appeal from the judgment of the pope to that of a council. But Vatican I explicitly rejects the legitimacy of such appeals.

(iv) Constance simply affirms that it is necessary for the pope to obey the council in matters of faith. Vatican I solemnly declares the *ex cathedra* definitions of the pope on matters of faith and morals to be infallible, irreformable of themselves.

Intimidating, no doubt, but are these contradictions any more than apparent? We must remember that it is not sufficient to base our interpretations of conciliar decrees simply on their "obvious sense". They must be studied in their historical context, in the light of the conciliar debates which helped produce them, in the light of the changes they underwent in their several drafts

165

as a result of those debates, in the light of the explanations appended to them and the commentaries written about them immediately after their promulgation—especially if any of those commentaries were accorded quasi-official status. If this is done, it is easy enough to see how the gap between the thinking of the two councils can be narrowed.

Thus, in the case of Vatican I, it has become fashionable, and properly so,[19] to stress the extent to which the final definition of infallibility fell short of the initial hopes of hard line "infallibilists" like Manning and Veuillot, and the degree to which it circumscribed the exercise of papal infallibility within certain narrowly defined limits. Again, it is frequently pointed out that the conciliar debates on the infallibility decree reveal the last-minute addition of the notorious clause *non autem ex consensu Ecclesiae* to have been intended to exclude the Gallican notion that no papal definition could claim infallibility, unless, *concomitantly* or subsequently, the bishops ratified it by according it their consent. It was not intended, therefore, to identify the infallible magisterium with the pope alone or to suggest that he was free to define a doctrine without making every effort to take into account the mind of the Church. And historical material was introduced into the preamble to the definition in order specifically to quiet minority fears on this score.[20]

Similarly, in the case of the primacy definition, we are reminded that the third paragraph of the chapter explicitly safeguards the powers of the bishops, indicating that they are not to be regarded simply as delegates of the pope.[21] This point was underlined still further by the collective declaration which the German bishops issued in 1875 and to which Pius IX gave his

19. See the analyses in Roger Aubert, "L'ecclésiologie au concile de Vatican," in B. Botte *et al., Le Concile et les Conciles: Contribution à l'histoire de la vie conciliaire de l'église* (Paris, 1960), pp. 245-284; Küng, *Structures,* pp. 229-249, 352-377 (bibliographies of recent literature on pp. 232, n. 9, and 366, n. 29); Dom Cuthbert Butler, *The Vatican Council: 1869-70,* ed., Christopher Butler (Westminster, Md., 1962).

20. Denzinger and Schönmetzer, § 3069; p. 600.

21. *Ibid.,* § 3061; p. 598.

solemn approval. And the teaching of Vatican II, reaffirming the primacy-definition of Vatican I but placing it side by side with the doctrine of collegiality, should surely remove any lingering doubts on this score. Attention, finally, should be drawn to the fact that the original drafters of the primacy definition, when citing in the preamble the Florentine decree on papal primacy (to the effect that the pope, as successor of Peter, holds from Christ the full power of feeding, ruling and governing the whole Church), omitted the concluding words: "as also is contained in the acts of the ecumenical councils and in the sacred canons." [22] But this important qualifying formula was restored in the final version, and, significantly enough, was restored at the request even of certain members of the majority group.[23]

Constance, of course, presents its own difficulties. The events preceding the acceptance by the council fathers of the final version of *Haec sancta* reveal that it was their purpose in that version to strengthen and not to weaken the limitations which it imposed upon the pope.[24] But it is still possible to narrow the gap between the thinking of the two councils by stressing the extent to which *Haec sancta* was the product of emergency conditions and designed to make possible a resolution in the case of conflict between pope and council. Whereas Vatican I was concerned with normal conditions in the Church, Constance directed its attention to the extraordinary, borderline, crisis situations. The relationship between the two councils, then, may well be one of complementarity rather than contradiction. If *Haec sancta* subordinates pope to council in matters of faith it should be remembered that even the moderate Conciliarists whose thinking it reflects were not concerned with *ex cathedra* papal definitions, since, at the time, the doctrine of papal infallibility was not widely held. It should be remembered, too, that these same

22. ". . . *quemadmodum etiam in gestis oecumenicorum conciliorum et in sacris canonibus continetur,*" Denzinger, and Schönmetzer, § 3059; p. 598.
23. Aubert, "L'ecclésiologie au concile du Vatican," 273, n. 52.
24. See Paul de Vooght, *Les Pouvoirs du Concile et l'autorité du pape* (Paris, 1965), pp. 29 ff.

moderate Conciliarists were themselves at pains to avoid denying that the pope possessed the plenitude of power in the Church. Finally, Vatican I's approving citation of the Florentine primacy decree along with its important qualifying clause might be taken to open the way to an inclusion of *Haec sancta* among those "acts of ecumenical councils" which are apparently to restrict the range of papal power.

And so on. It would be possible to elaborate, but I would be less than candid if I allowed myself to give the impression of finding at all convincing such desperate attempts at rapprochement. On the question of the primacy, although the Greek form of the qualifying clause (which is the one that the Greeks at Florence accepted, most of them being ignorant of Latin) is somewhat ambiguous and can be read as being restrictive of the papal authority, the Latin is not, and certainly does not seem to have been understood as restrictive by the fathers of Vatican I.[25] In any case, that qualifying clause had been inserted in the Florentine decree on the insistence of the Greeks who no more thought of Constance as one of the ecumenical councils in question than did the majority at Vatican I. That majority, moreover, was adamantly anti-Gallican. When the Bishop of Oran quoted a theologian to the effect "that the Pope could be judged by a Council if as a private doctor he fell into heresy", he was interrupted first with laughter, then with "murmers".[26] There seems to have been no room in the thinking of the fathers for the notion of the moderate Conciliarists that the pope in some sense shared the fullness of power with the Church as a whole or with the council representing it. The canon attached to the decree seems explicitly to exclude such a notion, and the accuracy of this appraisal is vindicated by the fact that we know the relevant formulas in that canon to have been included with the explicit purpose of rejecting the traditional Gallican arguments put forward by Bishop Maret, to the effect that the pope was a constitu-

25. See Butler, *The Vatican Council*, pp. 371-372.
26. In the debate on the primacy, see Butler, *The Vatican Council*, p. 339.

tional rather than an absolute ruler.[27] In his final exposition before the voting took place, Zinelli, reporter of the Deputation on Faith, stated explicitly that the power in the Church given to Peter was "truly full and supreme", "full in that it cannot be forced by any human power superior to it, but only by natural and divine law".[28] And the primacy decree, it should be recalled, was unapposed even by the minority group at the council.

Nor does it help to approach the matter via Constance. *Haec sancta* was concerned with the authority, not only of Constance but also of "any other lawfully assembled council", and on matters relating not only to faith or schism but also to reform. It envisaged the exercise by the council, therefore, of something more continuing than a merely emergency authority over the pope. This impression is strengthened by the later passage of *Frequens* and by the thinking of the moderate Conciliarists themselves. Nor, again, turning to the question of infallibility, does it help to point out that these men did not ascribe an infallible teaching authority to the pope. For neither did some of them ascribe such a prerogative to the general council, and yet they were still insistent that the pope was subordinate to the council in matters of faith. In any case, the adamant refusal of Bishop Gasser, representing the *Deputation on the Faith,* to admit that it was "absolutely necessary" that the pope consult the bishops before proceeding to an infallible pronouncement (a refusal endorsed, it would seem, by Vatican II in the very context of its discussion of collegiality),[29] would itself serve to render unbridgeable the gulf between the thinking of Constance and Vatican I on the exercise of the supreme magisterium.

These last remarks would seem to suggest that all is lost. But

27. Aubert, "L'ecclésiologie au concile du Vatican," 270; cf. Butler, *The Vatican Council,* pp. 98-99.

28. J. Mansi, *Sacrorum conciliorum nova et amplissima collectio* (31 vols.; Florence, 1759 ff.); continued in new 60-volume edition by L. Petit and J. B. Martin (Paris, 1895 ff.), LII, 1108 ff.; cited in Küng, *Structures,* p. 234.

29. *Constitution on the Church,* ch. 3, § 25; in Walter M. Abbott, ed., *The Documents of Vatican II* (New York, 1966), pp. 48-49.

is it? We have seen, it is true, that the "obvious sense" of *Haec sancta* would seem to contradict directly the "obvious sense" of the third and fourth chapters of *Pastor aeternus*. We have seen, too, that a study of those decrees in their historical context and in the light of the thinking of those who framed them does little to blunt the sharp edges of that contradiction. But we have yet to take into account the possibility that what is involved may still be a case of doctrinal development. Moreover, even if that possibility seems remote, to give up at this point and simply to concede the existence of so embarrassing a contradiction is clearly to leave oneself open to the charge of excessive "literalism" or "hermeneutical primitivism". And if this last charge is as devastating dialectically as it is intimidating linguistically, it is surely at all costs to be avoided.

Certainly, the matter of hermeneutical principles is likely to be the central issue here. No one would want to deny the reality of doctrinal development. Nor, today, would one wish to overlook the fact that councils have sometimes not hesitated to modify the dogmatic formulations of earlier general councils. Thus the Council of Florence modified the definition of the Council of Lyon (1274) concerning the procession of the Holy Spirit, making possible thereby the rapprochement between Greeks and Latins.[30] Similarly (though without signalling the fact), Vatican II modified some of the formulations of Trent.[31] But these cases involve the introduction of certain precisions or of cautious emendations of earlier formulations because of changes in the state of our historical knowledge. They do not involve outright abrogation of the earlier decrees—and that, given the explicitly anti-Gallican motivation of the majority leaders at Vatican I, would seem to be the only way in which one could relate that council's definitions to *Haec sancta*. The only theory of doctrinal development that would help us here would be one which en-

---

30. Aubert, "L'ecclésiologie au concile du Vatican," 281, n. 68.
31. Küng, *The Church,* pp. 418-420.

visaged development as embracing radical discontinuities, or, to put it euphemistically, dialectical unfolding. And such is hardly the standard Catholic theory.

What about the matter, then, of hermeneutical principles? All would agree upon the necessity of going beyond an analysis of the final versions of conciliar texts to an examination of the successive earlier drafts, of the debates surrounding them, and of the thinking of the people involved, and so on. And all this we have tried to do in the case under discussion. But some would want to go a good deal further than that. After all, the meaning of a conciliar decree "is not simply identical with the understanding of those who had an immediate share in the definition". The precise meaning of a doctrinal statement and the one to which we are bound to adhere today is not accessible to us simply by a rigorous use of the historical method. There has to be a complex and delicate interplay between "the indwelling ecclesiological consciousness of the Church today" and the actual historical declaration to which alone use of the historical method enables us to attain. Hence the possibility should not be excluded that "in the light of a new ecclesiological understanding" we might be enabled to determine the meaning of the Constance decrees with greater precision even than those involved in framing them. A deeper understanding of the case might reveal dimensions that contemporaries themselves did not perceive. "In other words", paradox or no, "it might in principle be possible to understand the decrees better today than the fathers of the council were themselves able to understand them." [32]

This approach is not to be dismissed without reflection. If one is willing to pay the price it demands, one will be enabled not only to resolve the particular contradiction with which we are confronted, but also all other conceivable problems relating to

---

32. Helmut Riedlinger, "Hermeneutische Überlegungen zu den Konstanzer Dekreten," *Das Konzil von Konstanz: Beiträge zu seiner Geschichte und Theologie* (Freiburg, 1964), pp. 224-225.

the continuity of the Church's doctrinal teaching, as well as a whole range of related problems besides. This approach is of added interest at the moment because by adopting it Gregory Baum has been able to criticize Charles Davis's rejection of the absolute and exclusive magisterial claims of the Church, while, at the same time, sharing with him, and to a truly astonishing degree, what Davis rightfully admits to be "the same vision of the Church and the same assessment of what is going to happen to the Church through the changes now under way".[33] A brief glance at the precise nature of their disagreement should help us, therefore, to assess the validity of these hermeneutical principles, and, *a fortiori,* to decide whether or not we should apply them to the problem at hand.

Davis contends that "for Roman Catholics the pursuit of the present renewal inescapably implies a plain admission that their Church has been wrong in declaring these structures to be permanently normative and of divine institution".[34] If "the new understanding of the Christian faith" is to become dominant, it will have to dissolve the existing church structure. Baum disagrees. For him the new understanding is already on the way towards becoming dominant and the structure is revealing itself to be flexible enough to accommodate it. Proof of this is that "extraordinary institutional event in the life of the Catholic Church" —Vatican II—which was undoubtedly "the beginning . . . of a

33. Charles Davis, "A Loving Defense of a Church That Never Was," *National Catholic Reporter,* June 26, 1968, 9. This is a review of Gregory Baum, *The Credibility of the Church Today: A Reply to Charles Davis* (London and New York, 1968), itself responding to Davis's *A Question of Conscience* (London and New York, 1967). This whole exchange, completed by a letter from Baum (see below, p. 174, n. 39) is most illuminating. Davis's book is a most important one but is in danger of being criticized in Catholic circles more often than it is read. Happily, by taking it seriously and proffering a considered reply, Baum may help rescue it from this fate. Both of these men, by focussing the central issues so honestly and so clearly, have placed all of us in their debt.

34. *National Catholic Reporter,* June 26, 1968, 9; cf. *A Question of Conscience,* p. 29.

profound doctrinal reform" in that Church. Hence, he asserts, "the crucial difference between Davis and myself lies in the evaluation of Vatican II." [35]

To this Davis responds, in effect, that the differences in their respective evaluations of Vatican II stem from the differing fashion in which each of them handles the texts of that council. Baum's interpretation of those texts, he alleges, "is not based on sound and objective criteria." As a result, he (Baum) is "wide open to the processes by which an institution distorts ('reinterprets' is the usual euphemism) the truth in order to keep its authority intact". Or, to put it in a different way, "he . . . has no defence against the bias of his own warm loyalties." [36] And Davis cites several examples which, on close examination, do indeed reveal Baum to have forced or even distorted the meanings of some of the conciliar texts in his efforts to prove that the Church is already well on the way to becoming what he wants it to be. The most striking of these is his distortion of an eschatological reference in *Lumen gentium* "into a new definition of the Church on earth" [37]; the most poignant is his attempt to reinterpret the Tridentine doctrine of original sin as being in accord with his own—poignant, because of Pope Paul's subsequent reaffirmation of the Tridentine teaching in terms that clearly exclude any such reinterpretation.[38]

35. Baum, *Credibility,* p. 12.
36. Davis, *National Catholic Reporter,* June 26, 1968, 9.
37. *Ibid.;* cf. Baum's *Credibility,* p. 24; *Constitution on the Church,* ch. 1, § 2, ed. Abbot, *Documents,* pp. 15-16.
38. Baum, *Credibility,* p. 35; cf. Denzinger and Schönmetzer, § 1514; p. 367. Note especially Baum's assertion that "whatever the fathers of a council may have personally believed about the first man, they had no intention of saying more about the universal sin in human life than is revealed in the scriptures". But Pope Paul's "new Credo" on this point clearly assumes that what is revealed in the scriptures is not what Baum thinks is revealed; see the text in *National Catholic Reporter,* July 10, 1968, 7. Davis, *National Catholic Reporter,* June 26, 1968, 9, correctly concludes that the principle which Baum invokes "means that no past Council can ever be interpreted as having taught anything that is not in harmony with the present interpretation of the Bible". The principle underlying the Pope's

In his brief reply to these charges, Baum does not focus on these specific examples but contents himself, instead, with accusing Davis of being "too literalistic" in his interpretation of conciliar texts and of being, in effect, too simple-minded in his choice of hermeneutical principles.

The doctrinal witness of the Church is not a body of literature to be interpreted *solely* with principles proper to literary criticism. Interpreting this witness we certainly use the methods of literary criticism: at the same time we also affirm—and here is the difference—that this witness refers to an ongoing reality, namely God's ongoing self-communication to the Church in his Word. In order to understand the meaning of biblical and traditional texts *today* we have to reinterpret them in the light of the Church's faith, created by this Word present in her life *now*.[39]

Now this is a breathtaking claim, and it is one which Davis had in fact already rejected with the remark that "Baum's principle of interpretation puts the truth at the mercy of an institutional ideology, where the institution may concede 'development' but can never admit that it has been wrong".[40] But a further clarification seems to be in order here. It is surely necessary to distinguish the hermeneutical principles appropriate to Scripture, which is certainly not a body of doctrine, and those appropriate to conciliar or papal doctrinal pronouncements. Although he himself makes no such distinction, I very much doubt if Davis would reject it. Nor do I think he would reject the validity of applying Baum's principle of interpretation to the Scripture—few Christian theologians would—provided, of

statement, on the other hand, would seem to mean that the Bible can never be interpreted as teaching anything that is not in harmony with the teaching of a council as understood at the time.

39. A letter to the editors in *National Catholic Reporter*, July 3, 1968 (italics in the original).

40. "A loving defense," *National Catholic Reporter*, June 26, 1968, 9.

course, that its use does not mean that the Gospel message is subordinated to the teaching of the present-day Church or to the meanings incorporated in its current structures. For that, of course, would be to substitute the Church for the Bible as the definitive revelation, and to Protestant charges that that is precisely what the Roman Church does, Catholic theologians (if not necessarily Catholic prelates) have nowadays become increasingly sensitive.[41]

What is at stake here, instead, is one's willingness or unwillingness to lump conciliar statements together with the Scriptures and to interpret *both* in accordance with the same hermeneutical principle. Baum insists that one must do so—despite the fact that conciliar doctrinal statements are fully human products in a way that scriptural texts are not, that they can lay no claim to the status of revelation, and that they are usually intended to clarify for us the meaning of the revelation itself. Davis insists, with equal force, that one must not. And this, it seems to me is the line that divides the two men. It is an extremely fine line but its consequences are immense. In the eyes of the official, teaching Church, it leaves one of these men a loyal Catholic theologian (ultra-liberal, perhaps, but still in good standing), while it makes of the other a renegade and an apostate.

All this, of course, immediately relevant to our own problem of the relationship between the teachings of Constance and Vatican I. If we follow Davis's hermeneutical principles, we must perforce admit the inadmissable—namely, the existence of an outright contradiction between the central contentions of two solemn conciliar pronouncements. If we accept Baum's, then it may still be possible, as Riedlinger suggests, to avoid that compromising admission and to dispose of our problem without

41. And that sensitivity is reflected in the carefully chosen phrases of Vatican II's *Dogmatic Constitution on Divine Revelation,* esp. ch. 2, § 10; Abbott, *Documents,* pp. 117-118; cf. Küng, *Structures,* pp. 352-366.

any unsettling reverberations. Or, indeed, any other comparable problem, for that matter. And therein lies both its value and its danger. Obviously, for any Catholic of strong loyalties, the *interior* psychological pressure to align himself with Baum on this issue is immense. But at what an intellectual and moral price! As Baum's own use of his hermeneutical principle in the two examples we cited illustrates so well, to accept that principle means, in effect, to be willing to make the past infinitely malleable and to subordinate history once more to dogma. And the stratagem that I have denied to conservatives throughout this book, I must equally refuse once more to their liberal critics.[42]

Let it be admitted, then, that the decrees and the ecclesiologies of Constance and Vatican I are in direct conflict one with another —and this despite the fact that both have to be regarded as meeting the requirements for dogmatic validity. What does this mean? It means no less than this: that the absolutist claims traditionally and currently made by the official Church for the magisterium cannot be sustained coherently by anyone who is ultimately willing to accept the evidence of history. It means that the claim to attach infallibility to *particular* conciliar or papal pronouncements must simply be dropped. Accordingly, it reduces also the claims so often made, and with such notable lack of restraint, for the binding force of papal pronouncements which *do not* lay claim to infallibility—or, because of their subject matter (as in the case of *Humanae vitae*), *cannot* do so.[43] It means, again, that conservatives no longer have to twist or reject the findings of the majority of biblical exegetes or to continue to manipulate scriptural texts in order to hold them to

---

42. See above, ch. 5, p. 134.
43. See *Constitution on the Church*, ch. 3, § 25; Abbott, *Documents*, p. 48: "This infallibility with which the divine Redeemer willed His Church to be endowed in defining a doctrine of faith and morals *extends as far as extends the deposit of divine revelation*, which must be religiously guarded and faithfully expounded." (Italics mine.) *Humanae vitae* grounds its moral teaching not in the revelation but in the natural law.

conformity with the obvious meaning of conciliar or papal doctrinal pronouncements in the past. It means, equally, that progressives like Baum no longer need put themselves in the
ludicrous and embarrassing position of having to distort papal
or conciliar pronouncements intended originally to *clarify* the
implications of revelation, in order to bring them into conformity with our current understanding of that same revelation.[44]
It means, indeed, that Catholics can throw off their peculiar
bondage to the recent past, that theologians, bishops and popes
can slough away their obsessive preoccupation with protecting
the "continuity" of papal and conciliar teaching, that no unsur-
mountable barrier need now divide the Roman Church from the
other Christian churches. At the present moment, finally, it
means both that Peter can be delivered from his chains and that
those radicals who have not given up entirely on the institutional
church can now permit themselves a measure of hope for a
genuine and thoroughgoing transformation of that church.

A drastic conclusion, no doubt, but is it not the conclusion to
which the modern philosophical perception of the essential historicity of truth also points with increasing insistence.[45] Is it not,
again, the conclusion that is most consonant with the witness of
the Scriptures, for, as Küng says, "the *a priori,* unquestionable
and *verifiable* infallibility of particular [doctrinal] statements
is something that is not directly demonstrable from the New
Testament." [46] Indeed, is it not the conclusion towards which
liberal theologians like Baum and Küng are themselves edging,
when, in their anxious attempts to do justice to the unquestionable
reality of change during the course of the Church's existence,
they increasingly stress the historically-conditioned and malleable nature of previous magisterial pronouncements. The trouble,

44. Which is precisely what Baum does with the Tridentine teaching on
original sin; cf. *Credibility,* pp. 34-36.
45. See, e.g., the remarks of Leslie Dewart, *The Future of Belief: Theism
in a World Come of Age* (London and New York, 1966), esp. pp. 126 ff.
46. *The Church,* p. 347.

177

of course, lies in the fact that it is a conclusion which demands of us what Charles Davis, in a recent exchange, demanded of the Scripture scholar John L. McKenzie, namely: the willingness to admit that the formulations of Vatican I's definition of infallibility are not merely "unfortunate" (countless Catholic theologians admit that), but that they are simply wrong. For if the linguistic distance separating the two words is slight, the psychological distance separating them is usually immense. And precisely because of this psychological distance, I would argue, it is absolutely vital that the coming Vatican III should itself be willing to meet that demand, to renounce, that is—publicly, unambiguously, and in the most solemn terms—the absolutist claims traditionally and currently made on behalf of the Church's teaching authority. So great a renunciation, so abject an admission of fallibility, so radical a commitment to honesty, would have an electrifying effect on the whole Christian world. It would liberate Catholic conservatives from the chains that bind them to an all too human past, it would free liberals from their bondage to an all too human present, it would leave all Catholics open, as rarely before, to the full, direct and devastating impact of the Gospel message. In an abysmally divided world that hungers, fears and hates, the Church would then be delivered from its unhealthy, debilitating and narcissistic preoccupation with its own identity and its own future, and freed to bring the whole of its formidable spiritual, moral and material resources to bear on the mission of mercy, relief and reconciliation. Then, truly, could it come to be the *lumen gentium* and the *sal terrae*.

(d) Tomorrow's Church

This brings us back, once again, to the matter of structural reform. I say this because the willingness or unwillingness of the coming Vatican III to make the great renunciation I have urged

178

cannot but determine the solutions it will give not only to the problem of the magisterium in the Church but also to the related problem of jurisdictional authority (and, therefore, of Church structures). There are strong grounds for believing that if this willingness is lacking, the new council, too, will remain unable, in the last analysis, to accept in their full intransigence the implications of the New Testament for the structural reform of the Church.

In this respect, Vatican II should serve as a warning. There is no doubt that the *Constitution on the Church* will stand as a great document and an historic achievement. And yet, as Davis has pointed out, any reader will immediately feel the contrast between its first two chapters and the third. For with the third it "moves into a new world, remote from the New Testament and dominated by an excessive stress upon juridical functions".[47] Again, pointing out that this chapter is "a highly controversial document as far as the various Christian Churches are concerned", Hans Küng argues that in it, "Vatican II does not claim to give an account of office which accords with the origins of the Church, or has a solid backing in exegetical and historical scholarship". It is not "analyzing the *essence* of ecclesiastical ministries, that part which is historical and permanent and decisively conditioned by the origins of the Church, but merely the historical *forms* of ecclesiastical office as conditioned by changing circumstances". All it gives us, in fact, is "a theological and pastoral description of the nature, order and function of the different offices, based on the *present* order of the Church." [48]

Because of this, although he himself does not say as much, he clearly feels impelled to downgrade accordingly the magisterial status of that crucial chapter. And yet, despite the evidence he adduces indicating that the theological commission may not have felt unsympathetic with this point of view, the Conciliar text gives

47. *A Question of Conscience*, p. 127.
48. *The Church*, pp. 419-420 (italics his).

179

no comparable indication. How could it, indeed, when it states that "this Council has decided to declare and proclaim before all men its teaching concerning bishops", when it notes that in so doing it is "continuing in the same task of clarification begun by Vatican I", when it indicates that the clarification it has in mind is Vatican I's teaching "about the institution, the perpetuity, the force and reason for the sacred primacy of the Roman Pontiff and of his infallible teaching authority", and when it adds that "all this teaching . . . this Sacred Synod again proposes to be firmly believed by all the faithful." [49]

Küng and other progressives may well wish otherwise, but it is hard to see how the fathers of Vatican II could have moved in any other direction, burdened as they were by the heavy freight of solemn magisterial pronouncements emanating from Vatican I. Without an equally solemn and public renunciation of the absolutist magisterial claims of the past, the members of Vatican III will be similarly burdened. The rehabilitation of the ecclesiology of Constance may help balance their baggage a little better, but their doctrinal burden will still be an appallingly heavy one, and on the particular issue of structural reform they will still be in a poor position to respond fully to the supreme example—that set by the Apostolic Church and communicated to us in the New Testament.

For it would be a mistake to think that it is only the ecclesiology of Vatican I that stands out as compromised when measured against that norm. It would be a grievous misunderstanding of the purpose of this book to conclude that my object has been to argue in favor of the substitution of the Conciliarist ecclesiology for that of Vatican I. Measured against our contemporary understanding of the Scriptural notions of ecclesiastical "authority", of ecclesiastical office, of the Church and the institutional structures appropriate to it, the ecclesiology of Con-

49. *Constitution on the Church*, ch. 3, § 18; Abbott, *Documents*, pp. 37-38.

stance, too, stands out as compromised—compromised by the heavy degree to which it, too, presumed the whole medieval and (as it now seems) unscriptural politicization and juridification of the Church.[50] The concern of the Conciliar theorists, it should be recalled, was with nothing other than the *potestas jurisdictionis in foro exteriori,* the public, coercive—what we would call—political authority, and with its exact location in the Church.[51] The concern of the New Testament, on the other hand, as its vocabulary so clearly reveals, is with the positive avoidance on this matter of ecclesiastical ministry of any link with secular modes of political authority.

If Vatican III, in its task of reforming ecclesiastical structures, is to be influenced by Conciliarist thinking, it would do well to turn not to the Conciliar theorists of Constance but to the much-maligned Marsilius of Padua, who, whatever his motivation and however damaging the concessions in matters religious he was willing to make to secular authority, was almost alone among medieval thinkers in perceiving that the type of public coercive power then wielded by the Church could not claim to be grounded in the New Testament.[52] Indeed, until the very recent past, it would have been proper to rephrase this last statement and to say "almost alone among medieval and modern Catholic thinkers". Modern canon lawyers continue to distinguish ecclesiastical power into a "power of orders" and a "power of jurisdiction". They continue to distinguish the power of jurisdiction into that which relates to "the internal forum" and that public coercive species which is exercised in "the external forum". The fullness of power which, in accordance with Vatican I, they continue to ascribe to the papacy is still a fullness of that *potestas jurisdictionis in foro exteriori,* which, as Conciliarists argued, he must in some sense share with the body of the faithful and the

50. See above, ch. 1, pp. 37 ff.
51. See above, ch. 2, pp. 71-72.
52. See above, ch. 2, p. 59.

general council representing it.[53] All of this, it should be noted, *despite* the fact that in the modern world the state has secured once more the monopoly of public coercive power, and has reduced the Church to the status of a private *voluntary society* comparable at law to other private corporate bodies devoted to the pursuit, it may be, of somewhat less exalted goals.[54] As such, despite the complex and labyrinthine redundancies of the canonists, the only type of public coercive power left in its hands is the power of moral coercion. And that is to say that the whole baroque edifice of hierarchical authority in the Church, however imposing it may be, rests ultimately (in human terms) on nothing less fragile than a common commitment shared in conscience by the individual members of the faithful. If a true realization of this important fact seems so far to have eluded the grasp of so many of those who hold positions of authority in the Church (as also of so many of those subject to them), it is in large part because of the success with which the pretensions of a universal Church, coterminous in its membership with society at large, have been sustained into the modern era under conditions of increasing pluralism by systematic resort to all the exclusivism and the defensive and disciplinary apparatus characteristic of the sect.[55]

Of course, there is every reason to believe that in our own age these sectarian stratagems are meeting increasingly with failure.

53. See above, ch. 2, pp. 71-73.
54. I am suggesting here that the Church possesses this status not in its own official self-estimation, nor in the depths of its true reality, but in the eyes of the state. In its own official self-estimation, if the canon law is any safe guide, it is still a "perfect society", i.e., an autonomous political society wielding jurisdiction. In the eyes of the state it is a voluntary society, a free, private, contractual association. In its true reality it is neither of these, for "it is an error to think of authority in the Church as a species of authority in general"; John L. McKenzie, *Authority in the Church* (London and New York, 1966), p. 12. The whole introductory analysis of the nature of authority (pp. 3-18) is very helpful.
55. Cf. Peter L. Berger, *The Sacred Canopy: Elements of a Sociological Theory of Religion* (New York, 1967), pp. 50 ff.

But even as they do so, the progressives who recognize and even welcome the fact are still impelled by the force of the tradition and by the burden of the magisterial pronouncements in which that tradition is enshrined and which they themselves are condemned to carry, to do much of their reformist thinking in categories that become meaningful only within a universe of discourse predicated upon the post-Constantinian politicization of the Church. It is surely unnecessary to elaborate on this point.[56] It is evident in the fashionable liberal pressure for "separation of powers" within the Church, in the demand for more representative and democratic modes of Church-government, in the desire to see the principle of subsidiarity applied in and guaranteed by specific legal enactments, in the push for revision of the Code of Canon Law, in the fact that Hans Küng, despite his repeated insistence that the practices of the Apostolic Church must constitute the supreme norm, would still seem to envisage the retention of so political a mechanism as the "matrimonial court".[57]

From all of this the reformers of Vatican III would be delivered if they were willing to make the great renunciation which I have urged, to abandon the absolutist magisterial claims of the past, to admit with full candor the historicity, the relativity, the reformability of all doctrinal pronouncements. For them they would equally be freed to recognize the provisional nature of all Church structures, the relativity and reformability of all ecclesiologies. They would be left, in other words, to confront the Gospel without impediment. They would be left, indeed, with a *true* ability to shape their reforms in terms of Küng's axiom that "one can only know what the Church should be now if one also knows what the Church was originally".[58]

56. On this point, see the persuasive critique in Baum, *Credibility*, pp. 193 ff.

57. Küng, *The Church*, p. 431. I mention this because I find it difficult to comprehend the retention of *formal judicial process* for matrimonial cases except in terms of a wholly politicized understanding of ecclesiastical authority.

58. *The Church*, p. ix.

What would emerge from their labors under such conditions? It would depend, of course, on what they made of a whole series of issues, such as the traditional claims for a scripturally validated Roman primacy or the question of the nature and meaning of apostolic succession, issues on which there is grave need today for exegetes and theologians to get together under conditions of openness that do not encourage them to place a wholly excessive reliance on the supple principle of doctrinal development. What would emerge, then, I do not know. But I very much doubt if it would be the Romanized version of the Episcopal system which some progressives seem to envisage, a democratized Church poised, in post-Ultramontane openness and under the guidance of skilled ecclesiastical organization men, on the brink of institutional mergers with the other great Christian churches. Rather than that, in the wake of its historic moment of truth and of humility before the Gospel, and sobered by its own de-mythologization of ecclesiastical authority, I would expect it to be discernibly "post-ecumenical", an ecclesial society of less traditional structure than that envisaged by most liberals, but more readily recognizable, more clearly institutional, more obviously rooted in the tradition than the localized and exclusivist experiments of the "free-church" people. I would expect it to be a radically open and pluralistic community, one which maintains a world-wide presence and the institutional structures which that necessitates, but which, eschewing rigid organizational boundaries, conveys its message and extends its compassion to all men. I would expect it, in fact, to begin to approximate to the model of the Church as "outer-oriented movement" which Baum has described and with which Davis has indicated his own enthusiastic agreement.[59]

For some the prospect of such a development will doubtless be an exhilarating one, a new Pentecost, a prospect, above all,

59. Baum, *Credibility,* pp. 196 ff.; Davis, "A Loving Defense," *National Catholic Reporter,* June 26, 1968, 9.

of hope. But we cannot close our eyes to the fact that for countless others it will appear less as a new Pentecost than as a new
Calvary. To these, confused by the clamor of contradiction in high
places, disturbed by the crumbling of the world they have known
and loved, threatened by the imminent disintegration of those
structures of meaning within which their very identities have been
shaped, it will, more than anything else, be a prospect of fear.
And what, in all compassion, are we to say to them? Charles
Davis concluded *A Question of Conscience* with the warning that
"there is a danger when much is at stake of imitating Bossuet,
who, according to Friedrich Heer, 'was a perfect man of the
baroque, preserving what he knew was false because he was
afraid of what might replace it".[60] If, more than once in writing
these pages, I have found it necessary to repeat that warning to
myself, perhaps I may be permitted to append to it the characteristically blunt appraisal of the late Pope John. "Fear," he said,
"comes only from lack of faith."

60. *A Question of Conscience*, p. 241.

Epilogue

In the Preface I suggested that it might not be improper to describe this book as an historian's attempt to open up a *via media* between the two paths that Charles Davis and Gregory Baum have made their own. If in the wake of the foregoing conclusions it may seem to some that the alleged *via media* departs in no way from Davis's route, I must insist that that is not the case. Davis and Baum, it will be recalled, are very much in agreement both in their general vision of the Church and in their perception of the degree to which it must be transformed if the current renewal is to be pushed to its logical conclusion. But Baum believes that with Vatican II this transformation is now under way, is already irreversible, and can be completed without the overthrow of existing church structures and without a sharp break in the continuity of Catholic teaching. And all of this Davis denies. For him the very logic of the current renewal imperatively demands so dramatic an overthrow and so drastic a discontinuity. If these do not occur, the transformation of the Church which Baum so ardently desires will inevitably remain stalled.

That I have considerable sympathy with Davis's arguments is, no doubt, very evident. He is certainly justified in his claim that Baum often "confuses aspiration with fact, texts with actions, and, consequently, overestimates the changes that have been achieved".[1] But at the same time, I continue to share at least some of Baum's hopes—though not, certainly, for his own optimistic reasons. The extent to which he is too sanguine in his appraisal of current developments, the events of the last summer

1. Charles Davis, "A Loving Defense," *National Catholic Reporter,* June 26, 1968, 9.

have served only to emphasize. My own reasons for sharing some of his hopes, therefore, are somewhat different in nature and they are in large part historical. The whole purpose of the central historical chapters of this book is to make clear what has been persistently obscured in the last century and more—namely, the fact that the Catholic ecclesiological tradition is less monolithic and more pluralistic than Davis and the vast majority of Catholics seem to realize. The view of Church history presented in Part I of the book leads me to argue that we may well be able to find in the riches of the tradition itself the resources necessary to open up the way for the transformation of the Church that is so desperately needed. And an appraisal of the changes in attitude being wrought by the current crisis of authority in the Church leads me to believe that a willingness on the part of Catholics to recognize and exploit those resources, even if it is not yet evident, is no longer entirely inconceivable. Because of this, I venture to conclude that Baum's uneasy and ambivalent mediating position (one which he shares with many another progressive), while it is certainly open to severe criticism, deserves a little more sympathy than Charles Davis is in a position any longer to extend to it.

How convincing my case will be I cannot myself judge. That it is unflawed by weaknesses I do not have the temerity to assume. But I no longer find myself capable of responding to anything but its strengths. *That* task I must leave to my readers and critics, contenting myself now with anticipating what I suspect will be two general criticisms—directed, if not against my arguments, at least against my conclusions. Both will focus on the issue of "institutional loyalty", but whereas the first will emanate from a liberal or progressive standpoint, the second will be of radical provenance.

Why, my liberal critics will ask, given the fact that theologians like Baum and Küng are laboring so hard, short of undermining irreparably the doctrinal and institutional continuity of the

187

Church, to do full justice to the demands of modern exegetical and historical views, why is it that I must insist on the need to take the further step that cannot but involve the insertion of a radical discontinuity into the development of the Church, and cannot but entail for the mass of the faithful a good deal of confusion, disillusionment and anguish? Does sympathy with the plight of my fellow Catholics or loyalty to the past, to the richness, stability and antiquity of the Catholic tradition, does this mean nothing to me and demand nothing of me? To which I would reply that institutional loyalty must not be paid for at the price which a Baum must ultimately pay—the price, as we have seen, of shaping the historical truth to respond to the exacting requirements of an institutional ideology. Along with much that is wholly admirable, one of the continuities which the liberals would, alas, preserve is precisely the demand by the institution that such a price be paid and the willingness of the members indeed to pay it. Only by the painful and dramatic renunciation which I have urged will the necessity for making so destructive a demand be eliminated and the willingness to meet it be destroyed.

True radicals, of course, will not be very impressed with these remarks. Having gone so far, they will ask, why stop here? Why not admit the irrelevance of the institutional Church to the real problems of the world? Why not concede the fact that *all* ecclesiastical institutional structures have in the past spawned their own idolatries, have obstructed rather than promoted a true apprehension of the full dimensions of the Gospel? Does not my own preoccupation with institutional change, however radical, itself witness ironically to the fact that I, too, am responsive to that very institutional loyalty which has served to blunt the arguments of the liberals?

There is probably something to this charge and I would not want wholly to deny it. But, then, for me, loyalty is not necessarily a dirty word, nor yet wholly discredited by its deployment

188

in the tarnished vocabulary of the ecclesiastical "politics of joy". Despite its corruptions and its malformations, despite its arrogances, its Pharisaisms, its dishonesties, it is in the Church, after all, that most of us have encountered the Gospel. It is in the Church, too, that many of us have learned those counter-meanings which alone enable us to stand in judgment upon what, over the course of centuries, the church-institution has come to mean.

To being moved, then, by a certain residual institutional loyalty, I suppose I must confess. At the same time, however, I must also insist that it is not that factor alone which has led me to adhere to the position for which I have argued. I have been moved also (and rather) by a conviction that a faithfulness to those truly human values which are the values of the Gospel must finally take precedence, not only over institutional ideologies—so well entrenched but nowadays so heavily bombarded —but also over those newer anti-institutional ideologies which are not necessarily as humanizing or as liberating as the insistence of their negations would have us believe. The Roman Catholic Church is a formidable presence on the face of the earth. It will not simply go away if we choose to cut our losses and to turn our backs on it. It disposes of immense amounts of property, wealth, power and influence. More important than that, it conveys at one level or another, and for millions of people, the structures of meaning in terms of which they shape their lives. One can hardly overestimate the good a reorganized, purified and revitalized Church could do, especially during the decades ahead when the problems of world poverty and world hunger seem destined to throw down a harrowing and imperative challenge to the selfishness and complacency of the post-Christian West. Equally well, one can hardly overestimate the damage it is likely to do, both in the lives of individuals and in the world at large, if the progressive reformers give up, if renewal is allowed to flag and if the church is "left to be run as it is". It has yet to be established, in other words that the world at large can easily sustain the luxury of too many drop-outs from Catholicism. Certainly, the mass of Catholics will suffer from such a development, for it seems likely to leave them bereft of any leadership but that of the ecclesiastical organization men who daily proclaim their own bankruptcy to an increasingly incredulous world. Even at a time when a healthy and imperative moral summons has gone out to all Christians calling them to turn from a cozy preoccupation with matters denominational and parochial to a greater involvement in the trials and tribulations of the secular city, there would surely be something seriously lacking in our compassion if we abandoned to their fate those whom Martin Marty has called "our own slow-moving fellow believer". Would we not do well to remind ourselves, from time to time these days, that the neighbor whom the Gospel exhorts us to love does not necessarily have to appear in the guise of the Samaritan or the Gentile? Is it not conceivable, after all, that he may well belong also to the fellowship of the Synogogue?